THE
RACE
CONCEPT

THE
RACE
CONCEPT

MICHAEL BANTON
AND
JONATHAN HARWOOD

PRAEGER PUBLISHERS
NEW YORK

Published in the United States of America in 1975
by
Praeger Publishers, Inc.
111 Fourth Avenue, New York, N.Y. 10003

© 1975 in London, England,
by
Michael Banton and Jonathan Harwood

LIBRARY OF CONGRESS CATALOGING IN PUBLICATION DATA

Banton, Michael P.
  The race concept.

  Includes index.
  1. Race. I. Harwood, Jonathan, joint author.
II. Title.
GN280.B36   572   74-30995
ISBN 0-275-33660-3
ISBN 0-275-85240-7 pbk.

PRINTED IN THE UNITED STATES OF AMERICA

CONTENTS

ACKNOWLEDGEMENTS

The authors wish to thank Professor G. H. Beale, FRS, Mr Terence Walbe, Dr Heide Ingenohl Harwood, and Dr Jonathan Harwood's former colleagues at the Science Studies Unit, University of Edinburgh, for commenting upon some of this material in draft form.

INTRODUCTION

The astronaut in a space capsule can look at the earth and see that it is a single unit. We know that geologically there has been one world for as long a period as most people can conceive. But from a social standpoint it is only in the last 100 years that we have had one world. The process whereby the major powers stretch out their tentacles and bring every part of the inhabited globe into the system of world trade and political rivalry is still not completed. Part of this process is the astonishing improvement in communication. People can now travel in a few hours distances that a century ago would have taken weeks, and the mass media can bring them in a few hours pictures and reports of events in the most distant places.

If people are to comprehend what is going on in Vietnam, South Africa or Northern Ireland, they must be able to think about the contending groups in terms which they understand. Often people want to know which side, if any, they should support in such struggles. To do this they must have a set of categories which will enable them to classify the parties. Only then can they say who is contending against whom.

In earlier times the most general categories used in the West were religious. Europeans saw themselves as Christians in opposition to Jews, Muslims and pagans. The differences were not just of faith, for political and economic pressures lay behind them, but relations between peoples were often expressed in religious categories. Then in the last 200 years three new sets of categories were developed in quick succession: those of nation, race and class. Nationalism was a European movement which

7

gathered strength throughout the nineteenth century and which utilised ideas of racial affinity. To come to terms with European pressures, peoples overseas had to make themselves into nations and join a world political system based on the principle of nationality and organised in bodies such as the League of Nations and the United Nations. The notion that every man has a nationality and should be governed as a member of a nation was something invented in Europe and then forced on the rest of the world. Europe rose to pre-eminence by a process of economic growth with which was associated a change in social structure and the appearance of distinctive class relations. With the extension of European influence some features of its social structure were exported. Conceptions of class have been elaborated in Europe and many Europeans now seek to interpret in this light developments in the rest of the world, although the patterns of solidarity and opposition in the Third World are often different from those in the industrial countries. With economic growth the resemblances will doubtless grow and if the peoples of the Third World see their position in class terms the process will be the more rapid.

These developments in the use of the ideas of nation and class have their parallels in respect of race. As a way of categorising people, race is based upon a delusion because popular ideas about racial classification lack scientific validity and are moulded by political pressures rather than by the evidence from biology. Nor are beliefs about race yet a basis for political organisation comparable to beliefs about nationality. Nevertheless there are similarities between the three kinds of category close enough to be worth reflecting upon. There are also similarities in the ways they have been developed. For race was a kind of classification invented by Europeans first to press the political claims of groups within European countries; then to represent the relations between these countries; only later when the potentialities of this way of labelling people had been extended and biological theories integrated with social ones, was it imposed upon the rest of the world.

Chickens, of course, come home to roost. The Third World

has accepted the tenets of nationalism, formed itself into national units and now uses nationalism to limit the power of Europe. Doctrines of class play an important part in ideological attacks upon European trading practices. The appeal to race is used to persuade black, brown and yellow peoples to co-operate against policies identified with the whites. Europeans racialised the rest of the world, but if peoples elsewhere accept this kind of classification they can use it against its inventors. Nor is the chain of action and reaction limited to relations between Europe and the Third World. There is a tendency for conceptions formulated in the most powerful countries to be forced upon the less powerful. Doctrines, slogans and tactics formulated in racial struggles in the United States are utilised in other western countries, many of which have national, class and racial divisions within their boundaries. The formation in Israel of a group calling itself Black Panthers is but one piquant example of this sequence.

It has been said that the study of race, like the theory of numbers, is something which drives men mad. But the study of race will derange only those who accept as an initial assumption that everybody belongs to some race, so that a complete and meaningful classification is theoretically possible. In truth one of the attractions in studying race is that it leads the student into so many intellectual pastures. It has to be studied his-torically, for the various meanings the word has acquired can be understood in no other way. Current notions of race are an integral part of the history of western Europe, drawing upon many aspects of that story. These notions cannot be separated from the rest of that history and attributed to single 'factors' like capitalism, colonialism, biological error or personal prejudice. The sources of popular imagery concerning race are very diverse and the interrelations between their growth and con-temporary political affairs are far too complex for the whole historical sequence to be explicable in simple terms. Race has also to be studied biologically, and this takes the reader into several fields which are often kept apart from each other. He needs to understand a little of comparative anatomy as it was studied in the nineteenth century, a little evolutionary theory, a little genetics, a little biochemistry and now a little ethology. Race has moreover to be studied in its social context so that the student appreciates why racial classifications evoke so much emotion, and how they can be entangled in, and exploited by, political struggles. On the frontier between biological and social study the student must have some grasp of the reasoning behind the psychologists' use of intelligence tests and the ethologists' extrapolations from the behaviour of animal species. This is so wide a range of fields that the student often has to be protected against the specialist who wants to drill him in more history, more genetics or more psychology than he has stomach for.

We have tried to take the side of the student against the specialist and to bring together the bare essentials from many of these fields. We have not tried to cover them all, but thought principally of the university student about to start in one of the social sciences, geography, psychology, social anthropology or sociology, and who usually needs a better grounding in the biological presuppositions of the textbooks he uses. Not only are these questions important to his subject but they are of critical significance in world politics and any progress towards a solution of what is often loosely and misleadingly called the race problem requires a better informed public opinion. Every educated person should have some understanding of the extent to which the differences between men and peoples can be explained as the outcome of their physical inheritance. If skin colour, hair form and physique are inherited, surely much else is inherited too? If the environment exercises a selective influence favouring individuals with a natural resistance to local diseases, surely it similarly favours certain mental characteristics? Is the concept of race one that needs to be taken seriously as an explanation of behaviour? Or is it basically a mystification elaborated by Europeans to justify their plundering the lands of weaker peoples? Indeed, what *is* the contemporary understanding of the race concept?

This book is conceived in the belief that no one can properly understand the contemporary concept of race by studying only what biologists now affirm. For thousands of years writers have described men as members of particular families, clans, tribes: as citizens of cities and states, as belonging to peoples distinguished by their language, dress and customs. It was only in the nineteenth century that they started to describe men as belonging to races and to maintain that differences between men and peoples stemmed from race. It was then said that some men belonged to races which had an inborn tendency to expand their territory and rule over others who belonged to lesser strains and from whom less could be expected. The peoples of Africa, of the Pacific, of the Latin American highlands and the Borneo jungles, who had not invented the wheel, found out how to make gunpowder or assembled libraries of written knowledge, were regarded as 'backward'. The backwardness of peoples was explained by a combination of the ideas of race and evolution. A simple technology might be the best one for maintaining life on a small island or in a restricted environment, but Europeans did not see it that way. They thought that the 'simpler' peoples were backward because their mental abilities were limited. Their races had not travelled so far along the path of evolution.

This new way of thinking was immediately challenged, but Darwin's discoveries seemed to support it. Towards the end of the nineteenth century and in the beginning of the twentieth, doctrines of race became more influential but controversy continued. As the scientific understanding of heredity progressed, it became apparent that the simple nineteenth-century concept of race was not compatible with the theory of evolution. Eminent scientists argued that as the concept of race caused so much misunderstanding while possessing relatively little scientific value, it would be best to abandon it altogether. Though they advanced some very valid criticisms they have not won many of their colleagues over to their point of view.

If an authority on biological subjects were to try to explain to a popular audience what scientists at present believe concerning the nature of race he would get into difficulty if he limited himself to ideas and propositions that are accepted. He would have to refer also to discarded ideas and explain why they have been rejected, for the layman has heard the drums and canons of the distant battle and many of these ideas, often in over-simplified form, have entered his mental world. They cannot be ignored. It is no use trying to spread over the top of them a layer of contemporary scientific views, for they will come up like weeds through concrete. We think it necessary for the reader to know how, why and when the concept was introduced, what has been claimed for it in the past and how it relates to later ideas if he is to appreciate what all the current dispute is about. The book, therefore, seeks to tell the story of a controversy: how it began, why it has been so violent, how the ground has shifted between anthropology, sociology, psychology and now ethology.

Chapter 1

THE CONCEPT POPULARISED

The career of the race concept begins in obscurity, for experts dispute whether the word derives from an Arabic, a Latin, or a German source. The first recorded use in English of the word 'race' was in a poem by William Dunbar of 1508, in which he referred to 'bakbyttaris of sindry racis' (backbiters of sundry races). During the next three centuries the word was used with growing frequency in a literary sense as denoting simply a class of persons or even things. Thus John Bunyan prefaces *The Pilgrim's Progress* (1678) by saying that he had been writing 'of the Way and Race of Saints' and a little over 100 years later Robert Burns could address the haggis as the 'chieftain o' the pudding race'. In the nineteenth, and increasingly in the twentieth century, this loose usage began to give way and the word came to signify groups that were distinguished biologically.

The first published use of the word 'race' to classify peoples by skin colour, hair and appearance is that by the French traveller and physician François Bernier, writing anonymously in 1684, but his essay does not seem to have led others to make use of this concept, chiefly perhaps because most of the treatises in anthropology down to the end of the eighteenth century were written in Latin. When evidence from geology, zoology, anatomy and other fields of scientific enquiry was assembled to support a claim that racial classification would help explain many human differences, the race concept acquired a new authority and entered upon a further stage in its career. However, the three centuries that intervened were ones in which other changes occurred that were to increase the importance of the concept as a way of classifying the peoples of the world. This was the period of the European voyages of discovery first to America and Africa, of the gradual establishment of a capitalist social order and of the slave trade. These changes may well have favoured the development of systems of classification which emphasised the differences between men of different skin colour. It was also a period when political struggles within Europe caused some of the contending parties to formulate claims based upon theories about their historical origins. These theories prepared the ground for a more systematic utilisation of racial explanations and inspired historical romances which took them to a much wider audience. We will take in turn the effect of Europe's overseas connections, of internal struggles, and scientific advances, before sketching the developed racial theories of the mid-nineteenth century.

THE PROBLEM OF BARBARISM

Popular ideas about differences between peoples grew out of European contact with the Indians of America, with Africans and with other peoples further afield. But it is essential to appreciate that it was changes within European societies which stimulated the voyages of exploration and trade which made these contacts possible. Changes within European societies decided what it was the travellers went in search of and even to some extent what they saw. These changes also had a profound effect on the interpretation which the people back home placed upon the new reports that were brought to them.

Though prior to the eighteenth century there was no conception of race as a physical category, there was a basic idea, grounded in European thought, that black was the colour of sin and death. It seems to have its origins deep in human personality structure, for it was prevalent before the coming of Christianity and has been reported, too, of black African societies at periods relatively little influenced by colonial contacts. From early times European Christianity took over and utilised this association between blackness and evil, so that in medieval romances the enemies of the knights are commonly said to be black; in the earliest illuminated manuscripts the tormentors of Christ are painted with black faces; in the south porch of the Cathedral of Chartres, the executioner of St Denis is shown as negroid. Little wonder, then, that when Europeans first met black people, their minds were full of these prior associations.

The great age of English exploration in the century before the revolution of 1640 was, according to Winthrop D. Jordan, an age driven by the twin spirits of adventure and control. Society at home was in ferment. The upper classes were anxious about the apparent dissolution of social and moral controls, while 'masterless men' who once had a proper place in the social order were wandering about begging, robbing and raping. The loosening of controls released new energies and many men were out to make the most of their opportunities, at home or abroad. These were the generations which represented Africans not only as radically different in appearance and way of life, but also as people of awesome sexual appetite and potency. Some told stories of African women publicly copulating with apes, and their readers were ready to believe them. How far this was because Europeans knew little about apes and were misled by accounts making them seem semi-human, it is difficult to determine. It is possible that both authors and readers were unconsciously afraid that they themselves would indulge in frightening forms of sexual licence if they were to relax their hold upon themselves, and they assuaged their anxieties by attributing to Africans what they feared in themselves. Philip Mason has indeed suggested that the decay of a belief in a personified, physical Devil has been a much bigger factor than is generally supposed in the growth of race prejudice in Britain. 'For lack of a Devil, we had to seek some other image on which to focus that mixture of dislike and yet repressed desire that we feel for sexual licence, cruelty and malignity.'

By the eighteenth century the reports of African societies had improved in quality, the differences between men and apes were better understood and there were a substantial number of black people in Europe. It was becoming apparent in more and more respects that they were all too like Europeans and that perhaps when left alone they led a more innocent and uncorrupted life. Why was it then that they had not built the ships to explore the European coasts, that they had no books, no gunpowder, no horses and carriages? Philosophers began to distinguish between the kinds of society associated with different economic orders. Hunting and gathering peoples were distinguished from cattle-keepers and agriculturalists. Some writers later developed a classification of savage, barbarous and civilised societies. What distinguished the civilised society? One of Jane Austen's characters maintained that it was the refinement of ballroom dancing, but the technical criterion was usually the use of writing. What was it that explained why some societies were still in the stages of savagery and barbarism? Would European societies continue to progress or did they run the risk of relapsing? These were worrying problems to which there were no agreed solutions.

The traditional answer to such questions had been to consult the Bible, which contained the clues to God's purpose in creating the world and everything in it. God had created Adam and Eve, and ordained that their descendants should spread out. He intervened in human affairs to help his chosen people and punished evil doers by ordaining volcanic eruptions, floods and pestilences. Yet the Bible said nothing about men inhabiting the strange lands which Europeans were still at this time 'discovering'. Its explanation of why some men were black was difficult to decipher. The notion that the prosperity or misfortune of nations could be attributed to God's will was becoming less persuasive. For this was an age in which the scientific approach was gaining hold amongst a wider range of people and the nineteenth-century European distinction between natural science and the humanities was unrecognised. Systematic study was revealing marvellous regularities in the universe, in the botanical world, and in the human body, which displayed the glory of the Creator. Science offered man a way of coming to know God better. The Bible stopped with the life of Jesus.

Something surely could be learned from the course of history since that time?

There were basically two kinds of explanation which were developed to supplement that of the Bible. One was to explain the degree of advance of societies by reference to what were then called moral causes (and today might be described as cultural); the other was to attribute them to physical causes in the human anatomy. The great humanists of the eighteenth century touched upon the problem of social development at several points. Montesquieu, Gibbon, Ferguson and others were fascinated by the decline of Greek and Roman civilisation. Athens and the Roman Republic had many of the institutions they wished to see in their own societies, yet somehow corruption had set in. Were civilisations like plants that germinated, flowered and withered away? The study of classical civilisations inspired humility in scholars who tended also to be well aware of the many peoples within Europe still leading a very rude existence. Adam Ferguson, who can be counted as one of the earliest sociologists, grouped societies in three fundamental categories—savage, barbarous and polished—defining each category in terms of characteristic economic activities, patterns of social subordination and constellations of opinions. He thought the clue to progress lay in man's success in developing the social organisation appropriate to his environment. There were no innate distinctions between kinds of men, nor were societies bound to progress, for much depended on man's own efforts. The Scottish philosophers of the late eighteenth century built an intellectual framework for the study of the moral causes of barbarism which had a dominating influence until enthusiasm for racial interpretations upset its assumptions. For example, Sir Henry Maine's great book *Ancient Law*, published in 1861, starts with the observation that of all the societies known to history, very few have progressed to a higher plane. What was their secret? Maine found it in the relation between law and other social institutions. If the law was too rigid a society stagnated. If the law admitted too many exceptions or was too easily changed, the society disintegrated. Progress depended not on race but on gradually changing the law to permit social relations to be based on contract instead of status, or, in modern terminology, upon achieved instead of ascribed roles.

Physical cause explanations of the stage of advance of different societies also have their beginnings in speculations about the Bible. That book seemed to certify that all men were the descendants of an original pair and were of the same nature. But was perhaps Adam the ancestor only of the Jews? In 1520 Theophrastus Paracelsus argued that peoples found in out-of-the-way islands were different kinds of men, not descended from the sons of Adam and therefore outside the Mosaic record. This way of getting round the difficulty gained adherents over the years so that two schools of thought took shape: the monogenists, believing in a single origin for man, and the polygenists, who held that different races or tribes had been separately created. The opposition between these two schools was not as sharp as a twentieth-century student might expect, because at this time there was no agreement on the definition of what constituted a species. In the eighteenth century many naturalists conceived of the various kinds of life, both vegetable and animal, as constituting a great chain of organisms, each specimen of which could only with difficulty be distinguished from those which stood on either side as links in the chain. It was easy to accommodate to this theory newly emerging ideas of racial inferiority, for blacks could be regarded as links in the chain intermediate between white men and orang-utans.

It is probably no coincidence that the first major attempt to explain stages of social development in racial terms came from a West Indian planter, Edward Long, who wrote a *History of Jamaica* in 1774. Yet it must be remembered that the travellers and the men engaged in the slave trade were more conscious than the stay-at-homes in England of the basic similarities between Europeans and Africans. In 1789 sixteen recent visitors to West Africa reported to a government committee. Though most of them had been involved in the slave trade, none mentioned any assumed African racial inferiority as a bar to future development. Some West Indian planters set little store by supposed racial factors, but racial prejudice was increasing in the islands. Long drew on scientific writings to construct a rationale for prejudice. He asserted that blacks and whites were different species; that hybrids between the two were eventually infertile; that blacks were closer to the apes. Africans, in his opinion, were 'brutish, ignorant, idle, crafty, treacherous, bloody, thievish, mistrustful and superstitious people'. They had on their heads not hair but wool. They were inferior mentally and gave off a bestial smell. Their physical nature was fundamentally different from that of Europeans. Long was regarded seriously as a writer with personal experience of the subject and his opinions were quite widely quoted. Nevertheless theories of polygenesis and racial inferiority gained few converts even in the closing years of the eighteenth century when the slave trade was under attack. Those who defended the trade did not want the support of doctrines that conflicted with the Bible. The religious revival of this period and the reformers' disappointment over the outcome of the French Revolution were stronger influences upon educated opinion.

RACIAL ORIGINS

European nations were themselves composed of peoples who had come from different regions. Sometimes the lines of political tension coincided with those of origin, so that evidence about the different customs of the original groups could be used in political argument. Jacques Barzun has shown how an opposition between Teuton and Latin runs through much French historical writing from the sixteenth to the eighteenth century. In the last two decades of the fifth century, Clovis, ruler of a small Frankish kingdom, conquered Gaul and established a new empire. By the end of the seventh century the Franks and the romanised Gauls had been fused into a single people. Later writers asserted that the name 'Frank' meant free Kings ruled by consent of their people. French nobles used this doctrine to resist the claims of the sovereign while maintaining that because they were descendants of conquerors they were entitled to a privileged position above the common people. This version of history was countered with arguments that for the most part Frankish immigration was peaceful and that no special privileges were granted to leading families. Historians combed the writings of Tacitus and Caesar to see what these could tell about the original Frenchmen as if the earliest customs were the ones that held the key to a natural political order for latter-day Frenchmen.

A remarkably similar controversy can be found in English political writing of the seventeenth century. Faced by the ambitions of the Stuart monarchs to weaken the power of Parliament and rule by divine right, some defenders of the Parliamentary cause turned to the historical record. They maintained that the English were descended from the Germans described by Tacitus. Richard Verstegan in 1605 published a book in which he argued that 'Englishmen are descended of German race, and were heretofore generally called Saxons'. Tacitus had testified of the Germans that 'the authority of the Kings is not unlimited'; 'on minor matters the chiefs deliberate; on larger questions the whole tribe'; and 'the king or chief is attended to more because of his authoritative persuasion than of any power to command'. In England at that time the adjective 'Germanic' was not in common use. 'Gothic' was employed instead, sometimes to identify the Jutes but more generally to refer to all peoples of Germanic as opposed to Roman stock. Seventeenth-century writers drew upon the book of Jordanes, a sixth-century historian of the Goths, who represented Scandinavia as history's workshop in which was manufactured a succession of peoples who emerged to conquer and settle different parts of Europe. Scholars also puzzled over the prophecies in chapters 2 and 7 of the book of Daniel (which have been called the first philosophy of history). These chapters suggested that there was a sequence of empires: Babylonian, Medo-Persian, Grecian, Roman, and that next perhaps there was to be a 'fifth monarchy' presided over by Jesus Christ. This kind of use of sometimes recondite historical sources is kept alive today in the British Israelite movement who believe that the Anglo-Saxons are descendants of the thirteenth tribe of Israel and are the real chosen race. They trace their genealogy through the captivity of Israel in Assyria and the settlement on the Danube of two tribes calling themselves Getae (later the Goths). Here they link up with Jordanes's history, with the Norse history of Snorre Sturlason and eventually with the settlement in Britain in AD 449 of Angles and Saxons under the leadership of Hengist and Horsa. This is not an amusing diversion. It reminds us that men regularly seek to elucidate their present problems by elaborating stories about their origins. In this way they imply that the key factor is the line of descent and in so doing they strengthen the inclination to racial explanations.

Just as some French writers believed the Frankish age of Charlemagne to have been a golden age for their countrymen, so there were Englishmen who believed that the Anglo-Saxon centuries prior to 1066 had been such an age for their forebears. It was embodied in the myth of the Norman yoke resting on the Anglo-Saxon's neck. This is truly a myth in the correct sense of that currently misabused word, for though it claims to be historical its essence lies in its message about the nature of Englishmen. It implies that inequality and exploitation date from the Norman Conquest, that they were absent before 1066; and that by reversing the Conquest men could return to a life of liberty and equality. The ruling class is pictured as the descendants of an alien oppressing race, who have no right to be in the country and no claim to the obedience of Englishmen. This myth had its own appeal for those who would reform the Church, for they liked to think that Englishmen practised a pure faith before the papal grip tightened upon them. Equally, it could unite the third estate against the Crown, the Church and the landlords. This myth was first used in the thirteenth century, then rediscovered in the seventeenth. David Douglas observes that by many early English historians the Conquest was represented as a national tragedy, and even as a national disaster. He suggests that because it was seen as a cause for shame it was not used by Shakespeare as a theme for one of his historical plays. The 1066 story of conquest or perhaps colonisation, by an invading people, could easily be turned into a history of racial conflict and used to set a special stamp upon ideas of the origins of the English as a nation.

This did not happen in Britain until the nineteenth century. Then the notion of race was popularised in a series of historical novels which reached a wide audience and probably made people more receptive to the later writers who claimed scientific authority for racial theories. In his novel *Ivanhoe* (1820) Sir Walter Scott made an imaginative use of the legend of Robin Hood. The book's theme is that of the ill-feeling between the resentful Saxon peasantry and their cruel oppressive Norman rulers, summed up in the line of a supposedly old proverb, 'On English neck a Norman yoke'. Scott uses the word race frequently in the loose older sense of Bunyan and Burns, but chiefly to denote Normans and Saxons as peoples. He has his characters talk of 'my race' and 'thy race' as if they were conscious of belonging to races. Another popular novelist, Edward Bulwer Lytton, did the same in *The Last of the Barons* which turns on the conflict between 'the King, his Norman gentlemen and his Saxon people' nearly three centuries later. Lytton made frequent use of the racial theme in *Harold: the Last of the Saxon Kings* in which, for example, a Norman is made to say to a Dane, 'we Normans are of your own race'. Charles Kingsley followed with *Hereward: Last of the English* which is somewhat more restrained, but the practice was spreading. More than one generation of Englishmen were taught that they were a distinctive race blessed with political institutions deriving from their Anglo-Saxon heritage. A colleague of ours can remember a history lesson in a Lancashire infants' school about 1950 when the teacher told the class of the magic qualities of the English racial amalgam and went round the desks pointing out children who had distinctively Saxon, Norman and Celtic racial features.

GEOLOGY VERSUS GENESIS

Though the biblical doctrine that all men were descended from

Adam was the dominant orthodoxy at the beginning of the nineteenth century, thoughtful believers had long been uncomfortable about the questions it neglected. If men had been created alike, why were they now so different? Observation taught them that there was no great difference between generations. In 1506 King James IV of Scotland examined a child born to a Moorish servant at his court, apparently to see how closely it resembled its parents. In 1578 a geographer testified, 'I myself have seen an Ethiopian as blacke as cole brought into England, who taking a faire English woman to wife, begat a sonne in all respects as blacke as the father was . . . whereby it seemeth this blackness proceedeth rather of some natural infection of that man, which was so strong, that neither the nature of the Clime, neither the good complexion of the mother concurring, could anything alter . . .' Yet the Bible seemed to say that the races of men had become differentiated in less than 6,000 years or so. Archbishop Ussher had calculated from it that the beginning of time fell just before 23 October 4004 BC, Archbishop Lightfoot's computations took him to 9 am 12 September 3928 BC. A dissentient voice held out for 5411 BC, but even so it was hard to explain such great changes in so short a period. Some monogenists considered that where there was insufficient evidence it was best not to speculate. Others found a biblical explanation, like Lord Kames who maintained that the races separated after the fall of the Tower of Babel when the tribes had been scattered. The story of Adam's expulsion from the Garden of Eden is one which suggests the theme of degeneration so it was not surprising that some writers believed that the backward races had degenerated through their failure to obey God's laws.

The key to the debate about the differences between men therefore appeared to lie in the age of the earth, or, more precisely, the length of time that man had wandered on its surface. If man's history was a long one, this left more time for natural causes to have produced differences, though it was still difficult to explain why any such differences should have come about. For this reason there was a special excitement about the changes which in the early decades of the new century were occurring in the field of geology. The doctrine of catastrophism which held that changes in the earth were due to divinely ordained floods and volcanic eruptions was overthrown in favour of theories holding that natural agencies at work on and within the earth had operated with general uniformity through immensely long periods of time. When, with the discovery of fossil remains of extinct species, it became accepted that the earth was older than 6,000 years, this changed the framework of the anthropological debate.

It is one of our main arguments that the rise of racial theories cannot be understood without paying close attention to the influence of scientific writings. It is sometimes claimed that racial prejudice began with the discovery of America and the beginning of the slave trade. Europeans wanted to make a profit from buying (or capturing) and selling black slaves or having them labour on the plantations. To help them still their consciences they manufactured theories of racial inequality. At other times it is suggested that so long as the slave trade was regarded as respectable, it needed no intellectual justification. Only when it came under attack at the end of the eighteenth century was there a demand for one. We have found little evidence to support such simple arguments. Though classical antiquity knew no prejudice of the kind seen in the nineteenth and twentieth centuries, the seeds were already there when Europeans first came into contact with Africans. For a long time Europeans were far too confused, and too committed to a biblical frame of reference, to formulate any such theories, for there was no adequate basis for representing mankind as composed of distinct species.

The first systematic racial classification was that advanced by Johan Friedrich Blumenbach in his pioneer study of 1775: *De Generis Humani Varietate Nativa Liber* (On the Natural Variety of Mankind). Blumenbach wrote that there were five divisions of mankind: Caucasian, Mongolian, Ethiopian, American, Malayan, and added that each division was 'connected with others by such an imperceptible transition that it is very clear they are all related or only differ from one another by degrees'. He thought racial characteristics had no value in systematic natural history but could serve as tracer elements assisting the scholar to trace the history of populations. Another anthropologist who accepted the Mosaic account of man's origin was James Cowles Prichard, the leading authority on race in the first half of the nineteenth century. He submitted his MD thesis at Edinburgh in 1808. It was similarly entitled *De Generis Humani Varietate*. 'Genus' could be translated from the Latin in various ways: as 'kind', 'family', 'origin' and so forth. It was not certain which was best. For example, Prichard in 1826 wrote of the need to direct attention 'to the external characters which distinguish one tribe of men from another' in circumstances where 'genus' would have been used in Latin. It was therefore a development of some importance when, helped perhaps by its use in French, Englishmen came to use the word 'race' to denote divisions of mankind which were distinguished simultaneously as social and as biological units.

The writings of men like Blumenbach and Prichard were studied as carefully in the United States as in Europe. In the eighteenth century, white American thinking on the subject of race derived from the same traditions as that of Englishmen, rehearsed much the same arguments and based itself on the same books. The founding fathers of the new republic were uncomfortable because they knew that the arguments they had used in seizing their independence from the English could be used against them by the blacks. 'We hold these truths to be self-evident, that all men are created equal, that they are endowed by their Creator with certain unalienable Rights . . .' ran the Declaration of Independence (1776). They tried to resolve the dilemma by arguing that Negroes were not men, or not citizens within the terms of the Constitution. At this time it seemed as if slavery might be dying a natural death as white landowners and others became persuaded of the advantages— and relative cheapness—of free white immigrant labour. But with the discovery of the profits that could be gained from planting cotton and the invention in 1793 of a cotton gin, there was a sudden upsurge in the demand for slaves. Slavery took root. Clergymen like Samuel Stanhope Smith, the President of Princeton University, who declared that God had created men equal and that the Negro's colour was a 'universal freckle', were forced back on the defensive—not by political pressure from slave-holders but by the force of the intellectual arguments that the polygenists were mustering. Why *should* some men be white and others brown, yellow or black?

RACIAL TYPOLOGY

The eighteenth-century debate about man confounded two separate issues: those of origin and of difference. The monogenists maintained that because all men were of common origin they must be basically of the same nature. The polygenists contended that men were evidently not of the same nature and therefore they could not be of common origin. Darwin's work gave support to the belief that substantial population differences could develop despite common origins, but in the decade that preceded the publication of his theory there was a growing tendency to put the problem of origins to one side as insoluble, and to concentrate on that of difference. It began to look as if some of the variations between societies and between men were to be explained by moral causes, such as the sequence of historical events which gave particular peoples high morale, inspiring leadership, effective modes of government, and placed them in the most favourable environments. These were critical elements in a people's culture. Other variations, like the inheritance of skin colour, were to be explained by physical causes. But just how powerful in human affairs were these two kinds of cause compared to each other?

One of the most important names in the history of this controversy is that of the great French anatomist Georges Cuvier. He first signalled a radical application of physical cause theories in the chronologically convenient year of 1800. Writing instructions for a French expedition to the Pacific on how they should study savage peoples, Cuvier's advice constantly assumed that man's physical nature determined his culture or way of life. Five years later in a lecture series he expressed his ideas more systematically, arranging men in three major races: whites, yellows and blacks, in a way that implied a descending scale. 'The difference between individuals is even more marked than between races' he wrote. 'It is not for nothing that the Caucasian race has gained dominion over the world and made the most rapid progress in the sciences, while the Negroes are still sunken in slavery and the pleasures of the senses.' Different races had skulls of different shape. Yet Cuvier was a mono-genist, a man who thought that slavery was degrading for both master and slave and must be abolished. He conjectured that after God's original creation of Adam there had been a series of natural catastrophes, killing off many of the species, and that after the last one some 5,000 years before, the ancestors of the three major races had escaped in different directions. This was scarcely satisfactory since it still did not explain what had occasioned the differences of skull shape, skin colour and so on. In Cuvier's scheme the concept of type is more important than that of race. Underlying the variety of the natural world was a limited number of pure types and if their nature could be grasped it was possible to interpret the diverse forms which could temporarily appear as a result of hybrid mating. Cuvier's influence upon nineteenth-century biology was very great indeed. It made certain that many other writers would view with great respect his threefold racial classification and his doctrines of the permanence of type and the physical causes of cultural variation.

An American school of anthropology which owed much to Cuvier's pioneer work made its appearance in 1839 when Dr S. G. Morton of Philadelphia published a volume about the skulls of American Indians and then, six years later, another about Egyptian skulls. The second volume sold well in the United States because it contained evidence of differences in cranial capacity and suggested that Negroes had been slaves from the earliest times in ancient Egypt, implying that their subjugation was natural and inevitable. The implications of

Morton's studies were developed and popularised by J. C. Nott, an Alabama physician, and G. R. Gliddon, a publicity-seeking enthusiast with some knowledge of Egyptology. In 1854 they brought out a volume called *Types of Mankind* which maintained 'that certain types have been permanent through all recorded times and despite the most opposite moral and physical influences'. It argued for the polygenetic theory, stating that dark-skinned races required military government and that unless the superior races were kept free from adulteration the world would retrogress. Under attack from the North for its commitment to slavery, the leaders of the South might have been expected to welcome this apparent justification of their practices, but instead they turned their backs. There was no biblical authority for polygenesis. They preferred to rest their defence of slavery on St Paul's epistle to Philemon in which he returns the slave Onesimus to his owner. A better indication of the defences favoured by slave owners was the book *Cannibals All!* by the Virginian author, George Fitzhugh. He attacked the wage slavery of northern capitalism, insisting that southern paternalism made possible a morally superior way of life. Only with the abolition of slavery in 1865 and the appearance of black people as a political force did theories of biological inequality begin to acquire importance.

Cuvier's line of argument was developed in Britain by his friend Charles Hamilton Smith and his former pupil Robert Knox. Smith, in *The Natural History of the Human Species* (1848), suggested that when the last great catastrophe occurred it was the men and women living near the Gobi Desert who had survived and from there spread out as three major types: bearded (or Caucasian); beardless (or Mongolian) and woolly haired (or Negro). He too brought the history of Jordanes into his account of the Caucasians! The Negro's lowly place in the human order was a consequence of the small volume of his brain. Smith repeated Cuvier's ideas about type and the infertility of hybrids but added a new element when he wrote, 'the effect of employing Negro wet nurses, universally adopted in the tropics, may be suspected to have some influence on the appearance and temperament of white children. Numerous instances of external marks, and of qualities for good and evil, may be traced to the practice; for none of the same kind occur in Europe.'

In his book of lectures *The Races of Men* (1850), Knox advanced the same theory: that the various types were suited each to its own habitat and therefore unchanging. The ways of life of different peoples were determined by their physical constitutions, the study of which he defined as 'transcendental anatomy'. Though Knox's book was a poorly organised and unconvincing piece of work it sounded a new note, 'race is everything'; race determined the course of history and the behaviour of one nation to another. If the word 'racism' is used in its original sense to refer to the doctrine that race determines the culture of peoples and the moral or intellectual qualities of individuals, Knox's lectures are the first book-length racist statement. Yet the book was probably of less importance than Knox's personal influence, in his lectures to medical students and through his energetic disciple James Hunt who formed the Anthropological Society of London in 1863. This body sought to emulate the Paris Society founded by Paul Broca. It published in English translation a number of treatises on race by continental scholars, such as the lectures by Carl Vogt, a Swiss follower of Cuvier who believed that the sutures, or cracks, between the bones of the Negro's skull closed earlier than in white races, inhibiting the further development of the intellectual faculties.

While Knox's book was being read in Britain, and Nott and Gliddon were planning theirs in America, similar applications of the theory of racial types were being attempted by German and French writers. The most famous of these was Count Joseph Arthur de Gobineau's four-volume *Essay on the Inequality of Human Races* which began to appear in 1854. Like Cuvier, Gobineau did not challenge the belief that all men were descended from Adam. Like Cuvier he argued for the permanence of type while speculating that human development had passed through a series of stages and that in one of these the three major races had become separated. Gobineau was much less concerned about the biological aspects of human variation than the other authors we have mentioned. He passed on quickly to a review of the histories of the major world civilisations maintaining that they were the creations of different races and that race-mixing was leading to the inevitable deterioration of humanity. In his lifetime, Gobineau's work attracted relatively little attention but afterwards his arguments about the superiority of the Aryan race were used by the prophets of German nationalism. Some sociological writers have accorded him a more prominent place in the history of racial theories than his work really merits.

The middle of the nineteenth century saw the notion of race at the peak of its career as a scientific concept. It stated that the species *Homo sapiens* was composed of distinctive varieties and that the behaviour of individuals and groups was to be understood as determined by their place in this natural order. Those who insisted on the importance of race had achieved two things of great significance. Firstly the scientific world had accepted that in comparative morphology (the study of the shapes and structures of the human body) it was a valid procedure to distinguish a variety of anatomical types and to call them races. Secondly, the initiative lay with arguments advancing physical causes as the explanation of all human differences. *Homo sapiens* was presented as a species divided into a number of races of different capacity and temperament. Human affairs could be understood only if individuals were seen as representatives of races for it was there that the driving forces of human history resided. Racial typology was not at this time necessarily a politically conservative doctrine. It opened up a prospect whereby man might take command of his own affairs, and its advocates were bitterly critical of ecclesiastical attempts to restrain scientific enquiry. Racial typology threw on the defensive those who wished to explain the differences between peoples in terms of their environment, way of life and history. It drove a wedge into the Christian belief in the brotherhood of man. Prior to the nineteenth century, scholars believed that all peoples could progress. After the 1850s a substantial school of thought held that some peoples never could advance. Europeans were coming to believe that the divisions among themselves were small by comparison with the gulf between white people and other races.

The claims of the racial typologist for the universal priority of physical causes were never challenged on a broad front because after the publication in 1859 of Charles Darwin's *Origin of Species* the framework of scientific enquiry was transformed. Nevertheless the opposition, already apparent before Darwin, between two approaches to the study of human variation has continued. The social anthropologists and other social scientists start from the diversity in the human condition as it exists today, studying differences in customs, the relations between groups that are called racial, and the organisations which influence the patterns of human co-operation and conflict. They tend to select for study the sorts of problem which appear to be the outcome chiefly of social, economic and political relations, and in which the biological element seems small. The physical anthropologists and other biological scientists start from the laboratory or the controlled experiment. They select problems in which the biochemical component seems important. They hope to work upwards from systematic knowledge about basic elements to the explanation of ever more complex phenomena.

It is necessary that there should be two such approaches but they sometimes appear contradictory. Some scholars have tried to draw a sharp distinction between the race idea, as essentially a political phenomenon, and the race concept, as something in the realm of science. Others have said that the social scientist studies 'social race', which is defined by what people believe to be the nature of race, and that this is fundamentally different from 'biological race', which is something understood only by specialists in the life sciences. There is here a genuine difficulty which is reflected in an argument brought against the conception of *race* relations as a field of study. It is said that this field deals with groups that are socially defined and that it is confusing to identify these groups by an adjective, race, which implies that they are biological units. We are suspicious of attempts to cut a way out of the maze by representing biological and sociological research as fields whose subject-matter must be for ever separate. We argue that the use of the term race in both biological science and the everyday world needs to be understood historically. It is wrong to accept without examination the claim that racial classification is meaningful within biology. As our knowledge increases there will be many more phenomena which we will succeed in explaining in biochemical terms. There will be many more that we will explain in social terms. There will come a time when many of the present gaps between the theories of physical and social anthropology have been filled and it will be possible to measure the relative importance of physical and social causes to the appearance of particular conditions.

Another question remains. The theory of racial types was a fateful error which contributed significantly to Europe's imperial arrogance at the turn of the century and to the politics that entailed the murder of 6 million Jews. It was no ordinary mistake, so it is necessary to look a little closer into its origins. The reader should remember at the outset that 130 years ago biologists were ignorant of much that even the man in the street today takes for granted. Charles Hamilton Smith's notion of the properties of mother's milk is but one example. Educated people were then very ignorant about the formation of the embryo in the mother's womb and many believed that a person's character was determined by the shape of his head. If they could be wrong about such matters it is less surprising if they could be wrong about questions like the alleged infertility of hybrids which required careful research covering several generations. Biological studies were not well represented in England's four universities and Darwin never held a university post. There was no reason in principle for rejecting the proposition that race determined culture. It could have been true. Scientists are continually making mistakes but unlike Darwin they are today involved in an intellectual community which usually recognises them before they reach a popular audience. Criticism of racial theories failed to destroy them at that time not because the proponents of racial theories were evil, prejudiced men, but because the scientific community in the biological field was still very loosely organised and the world outside was eager to utilise the theories before they had won widespread scientific support. Charles Hamilton Smith was a former army officer who had taken up zoology and published his book as President of the Devon and Cornwall Natural History Society. Robert Knox was a former lecturer, a medical journalist with a small practice. James Hunt ran an institution for the treatment of stammering. Gobineau was a novelist and a diplomat. If they lacked scientific caution, and if (like Hunt) they publicised their ideas with vigour, it was because they believed they had discovered something of great significance. It is also worth recalling, as Michael Biddiss has observed, that the middle years of the century were a period when many scholars were seeking grand synthetic philosophies. Comte, Marx and Spencer were the outstanding examples, but there were many others (and sociology itself is a product of the movement). Gobineau attempted a similar synthesis, and so in smaller compass did the other typologists. It was not surprising if men at this time thought that in racial classifications there might be an avenue to such a grand understanding of human history.

It is sometimes suggested that the theories of racial inequality were produced because capitalists needed an ideological justification for exploiting black people overseas but this is not a persuasive argument with respect to the European writers. The links that such a theory postulates have not been established and the dates do not fit well enough. The theories preceded the conflicts of interest rather than following upon them. Signs of a more hostile attitude towards black and brown peoples overseas began to appear in the 1850s and 1860s. The events of the Indian mutiny (1857) were grossly misrepresented when reported in Britain and aroused racial prejudice. The controversy in 1865 over Governor Eyre's brutal repression of an apparent revolt in Jamaica had a similar effect, while the Civil

War in the United States and the continuing controversy over the claims of the black American had many repercussions on the eastern shores of the Atlantic. But the English national mood had not decisively changed by this time. In 1865 the House of Commons adopted the resolutions of one of its committees which recommended that there should be no further annexations of territory in West Africa; Britain should reckon on withdrawing from her colonies there, with the possible exception of Sierra Leone (then limited to the little peninsula on which Freetown had been founded). European involvement in Africa was slight and the classes which might want such a justification were not under attack on this account. Later on as European interests in Africa increased, and, with the extension of the franchise, the working classes were drawn into support for imperial adventures, there was a warmer welcome waiting for doctrines of white superiority, but that was a feature of a later period.

The main ideological influence upon the theorists of racial types was almost certainly not that of Europe's relations with black peoples but rather the tensions within Europe itself. In 1848 many European countries had been shaken to their foundations by a series of popular movements. The ruling and commercial classes were undoubtedly frightened. It seemed as if political power might pass to ill-educated inferior orders and the maps of national boundaries be redrawn. Racial doctrines were eminently applicable to struggles within Europe. To take just one example, in Knox's scheme the Austrian Empire was a tyranny of Goths over Slavs. The Hungarians were an intrusive element who would not long be able to maintain themselves in an environment to which they were not suited. Again, racial doctrines can be seen as a justification of nationalist movements seeking to head off the yawning divisions between classes.

The connections between class divisions at home and racial divisions overseas may have been more subtle than we yet appreciate. Philip Mason has argued, in an illuminating manner, that among the social changes of eighteenth- and nineteenth-century England was a growing aloofness on the part of the middle and upper classes. At the beginning of this period men took it for granted that they were not equal but behaved as if they were. By the end of the period the higher classes realised that members of the lower classes were not innately different and had consciously decided on a gradual extension of privilege and wealth. Yet they treated their social inferiors as if they were inherently unequal. Members of the lower orders were supposed to smell: they were kept at a distance and servants, for example, were not allowed to use the same lavatories as their employers' families. It looks as if there may have been an unconscious fear of social equality and as if economic growth gave the rich the opportunity to erect the social barriers they unconsciously wanted, in place of the old ones rooted in the feudal conception of society. It is possible that there was a connection between this growth of personal aloofness between the classes at home and the comparable increase overseas in the sense of a necessary gulf between the white rulers and their black or brown subordinates.

THE IMPACT OF DARWINISM

Within biology a new approach towards the question of race was made possible by Darwin's *Origin*, which cut down the false debate between the monogenists and polygenists and pointed to an explanation of gradual but continual change in man's heredity. *On the Origin of Species by Means of Natural Selection; or, The Preservation of Favoured Races in the Struggle for Life* (to give it its full title) was not about evolution so much as about natural selection, the means by which evolution was possible. Natural selection is the process by which those members of a plant or animal population which are best adapted to their environment contribute more to future generations than those which are less well endowed. The criterion of success is the number of viable offspring which members of a population leave after them. Darwin thought that inheritance operated by a blending of parental heredity in the offspring. If this were the only factor at work it should have made populations ever more uniform.

So he supposed that there must be occasional changes in individuals' heredity which could lead to variation in the population. This part of the theory assumed that the source of variation must be recent and that, to be effective, selection must be powerful enough to spread a new advantageous form very quickly before its value was lost by the blending that would occur in the next generation. This mistake led Darwin to present selection as a more sudden and violent process than we now know it to be, but it harmonised with his generation's rather bloodthirsty view of nature as 'red in tooth and claw'. This view in turn was used to justify the ruthless social and economic policies of a nation flushed by unprecedented economic expansion.

Darwin made no attempt to classify races, observing that the naturalist has no right to give names to objects which he cannot define. Yet he d d consider that some races were biologically inferior. In *The Descent of Man* (1871) he wrote: 'The belief that there exists in man some close relation between the size of the brain and the development of the intellectual faculties is supported by the comparison of the skulls of savage and civilised races, of ancient and modern people, and by the analogy of the whole vertebrate series.' He went on to quote approvingly an author who stated: 'Given a land originally peopled by a thousand Saxons and a thousand Celts—and in a dozen generations five-sixths of the population would be Celts, but five-sixths of the property, of the power, of the intellect, would belong to the one-sixth of Saxons that remained. In the eternal "struggle for existence" it would be the inferior and less favoured race that had prevailed—and prevailed by virtue not of its good qualities but of its faults.' Nations would be weakened if men's sentimentality prevented natural selection from doing its terrible work. This quotation reminds us that in England at that time, doctrines of racial inferiority were used more against the Irish than against black or brown peoples.

Darwin was a much more cautious man than the host of those who rushed in with speculations about how the Darwinian principles of heredity and selection might be applied to human affairs. These men formed a school that became known as social Darwinism. Herbert Spencer helped in its foundation though his views diverged from the main tendencies of the developing movement. One of the earliest and most interesting social Darwinist writers was the Austrian sociologist Ludwig Gumplowicz. He argued in a radical fashion for bringing the methods of natural science to bear on the problems of the moral sciences. He held that 'the means by which tribes became peoples, peoples nations, nations grew into races and developed themselves, is the perpetual struggle between races for dominance, the soul and spirit of all history'. As the social units grew in size so they created new myths and religions to help themselves onward. But Gumplowicz's vision introduces a theme that is new. Even the most ardent enthusiasts for racial classification had acknowledged that the various groups of men did not all fit easily into any simple scheme of types. Influenced by the possibility of degeneration they had been inclined to assume that there had once been a limited number of pure races, but that in the course of time mixing had taken place and given rise to individuals and groups of intermediate status. Gumplowicz, on the other hand, viewed pure races not as things of a vanished past; races could be new units which were in the course of creation. Antagonism between groups would effect breeding patterns and could produce a set of more distinctive races than had previously existed.

There were two contrasting elements in the social Darwinist conception of evolutionary change. The pessimistic one was best exemplified by the French writer Georges Vacher de Lapouge who maintained that natural selection operated to the advantage of the worst elements in the population. In war-time it was the patriots who were killed, not the cowards. In democratic societies the demagogue and trickster triumphed over the honest man. Charity preserves the weak, capitalism destroys natural aristocracies and the poor have most children. 'I am convinced [he wrote in 1887] that in the next century millions will cut each others' throats because of one or two degrees more or less of cephalic index [skull measurement]. This is the sign which is replacing the Biblical *shibboleth* and linguistic affinities, and by which people will recognize one another as belonging to the same nationalities and by which the most sentimental will assist at the whole-sale slaughter of peoples.' The optimistic element is represented in the work of the German anthropologist Otto Ammon who believed that natural selection was eliminating the weaker strain and that humanitarianism should not be allowed to impede nature's mechanism for improving the human stock. Ammon's work shows how the race concept—which earlier had been applied almost exclusively to national groups—could be applied to class differences. From measurements of peoples' heads he concluded that the Nordic division of the Caucasian race was characterised by tall stature and egg-shaped (dolichocephalic) skulls found mostly amongst the upper classes of his country; the Alpine people were short-legged with billiard-ball-like crania (brachycephalic) and they were found mostly in the lower classes. Class distinctions were Nature's way of seeing that human affairs are directed by those best fitted for the job. The idea of the selection of the fittest was a popular one at this time, but it rested on a circular argument so long as there was no independent assessment of fitness. Some groups obviously survived, but there was no way of being sure that they were the fittest.

At the end of the nineteenth century there was a bewildering variety of racial classifications. It seemed as if every anthropologist had his own. Some based their systems on differences of hair form and hair colour; others on skin colour, eye colour and eye form, stature, head form, nose form etc. The great weakness in these schemes was that no one was quite sure what races were to be classified *for*. A classification is a tool. The same object may be classified differently for different purposes. No one can tell what is the best classification without knowing what it has to do. The anthropologists of this generation were trying to sort out various kinds of men in the belief that before long other important things would be found to coincide with their racial distinctions. They could not know at the time that they were wrong in this. Only with the rediscovery of Mendel's work did scientists begin to think in terms of relatively stable genetic foundations (the genes) underlying the outward features like colour which previously had seemed more obvious criteria for classification. Slowly it came to be realised that perhaps race should not be seen as a concept in comparative morphology and that classifications should be based on the invisible determinants instead of the visible forms. This understanding was important in other fields also, for social Darwinism had been applied as vigorously to social classes as to racial groups. The Eugenics Education Society was founded in 1908 to publicise the dangers in contemporary patterns of fertility. The feeble minded and criminal were being drawn from the fertile lower classes whereas among the more intellectual classes the birthrate was low and declining. Within each occupational group the less intelligent had larger families. Education might counterbalance inheritance but it could not eliminate the less desirable genes nor multiply the more desirable. The prospect seemed alarming.

It takes time for scientific discoveries to be evaluated and digested. Scientists cannot always agree about the interpretation of new evidence, for it is sometimes ambiguous and confusing, especially if it upsets established reputations and patterns of thought. The public are inclined to believe what they want to believe, if they can claim enough justification to get away with it. Scientists are themselves members of the public and may be influenced by popular assumptions. Europeans in the late nineteenth and early twentieth century were very ready to believe stories about the superiority of the white race. There were historians who reinterpreted their national histories as the manifestation of the spirit of the Anglo-Saxon, the Gallic and the Teutonic races. There were novelists who found in race a mode of reasoning that lent itself to literary embellishment. This, after all, was the high noon of imperialism, the time of the first popular newspapers and of national enthusiasm for the building of battleships. People so glorified in the strength of the white race that a critic suggested that a new beatitude had been incorporated into the English religion: 'Blessed are the strong, for they shall prey upon the weak.' An American historian, William L. Langer, concluded that though economic factors were important in the growth of imperialism, 'the prevalence of evolutionary teaching was perhaps crucial. It not only justified competition and struggle but introduced an element of ruthlessness and immorality that was most characteristic of the whole movement.'

To draw up a balance sheet of European colonialism would not be easy. There were more important elements than the ruthlessness and immorality to which Langer referred. There is much to be said in favour of many colonial policies and many administrators, as well as much that can be said against them. Above all, it is impossible to compare what happened under colonial rule with what might have happened had it never taken place. But there is considerable evidence in line with Philip Mason's thesis about a growing aloofness on the part of British colonial officials in India in the latter part of the nineteenth century and in Africa a little later. In part this was doubtless because improvements in transport made it possible for more men's wives to join them and the British consequently withdrew into their own community. Yet some of the change does seem to have been due indirectly to the talk about racial differences. In West Africa the British had established a medical service with African doctors serving on a similar basis to Europeans. From 1902 regulations were enforced confining African doctors to a category with lower salary scales so that even the most senior African doctor could not give an order to the most junior white doctor. So many of the earlier discussions about whites, browns and blacks in West Africa had been couched in racial terms that this change—and others of a more general kind—must surely have been in some measure a consequence of an official acceptance of the doctrine that the British were a race as well as a nation.

In the early years of the twentieth century, Germany emerged as the main rival to Great Britain. Less was heard about racial theories because the British and the Germans were supposed to be of the same stock. In the United States, however, controversies about race became more heated. This time the centre of attention was not the supposed inferiority of the Negro but the tensions of immigration and the expansionist appetites of men such as A. J. Beveridge who, in 1900, lectured his colleagues in the Senate: 'God has not been preparing the English-speaking and Teutonic peoples for a thousand years for nothing but vain and idle self-contemplation and self-admiration. No! He has made us the master organisers of the world to establish system where chaos reigns . . . He has made us adept in government that we may administer government among savage and servile peoples.' Others expressed the fear that the country was admitting immigrants of poor stock from eastern Europe and southern Italy whose assimilation into the population would lead to a general deterioration. Californians feared the 'Yellow Peril'. Madison Grant was to claim that his book *The Passing of the Great Race* (1916) persuaded Congress to pass the Immigration Acts of 1921 and 1924 which until 1965 barred undesirable races from the United States by establishing a set of racially based quotas. Twelve out of every fifteen immigrants had to be from Britain, Ireland, Germany, Netherlands and Scandinavia. Japanese were forbidden. Social Darwinism was more influential in the United States than in Europe for it fitted in both with the attempts of American scholars, well in advance of most Europeans, to create an empirical science of society, and with the free enterprise ethic epitomised by William Graham Sumner as 'root, hog! or die!'. By the 1920s, however, loose use of the race concept was under strong attack in the United States, led by the anthropologist Franz Boas, and the story is one which belongs more to the next chapter.

The most destructive and terrible phase in the career of the race concept came in Hitler's Germany. An Englishman turned German citizen called Houston Stewart Chamberlain had published in German in 1897 two volumes entitled *The Foundations of the Nineteenth Century*. Their theme was that race is made by man, by the will of the people. 'Even if it were proved that in the past there never was an Aryan race, we want there to be one in the future' and the Germans were to be its genius. The book was publicised by the Kaiser and its themes must have been known to the young Hitler who came to pay court to the sickly Chamberlain in 1923. In the later exhortations of Hitler these ideas of the German master race, and of antisemitism, were to attain their most strident expression, while the windy fantasies of Alfred Rosenberg's *The Myth of the Twentieth Century* appeared to give them intellectual respectability (Rosenberg drew wittingly on Chamberlain and unwittingly on Vogt's idea of a 'raceless chaos' to write a 'race history' in which 'race is the externalisation of soul'). The universities all too quickly crumpled before political pressure to recast all their teaching in terms of the racial theories of a few professors who still adhered to a nineteenth-century conception of race. They did not limit themselves to anthropological measurements but freely attributed different kinds of temperament, political skill and virtue to the various races, edging delicately round problems of definition and ignoring the many inconsistencies in their speculations and the contradictions with recorded history. The stress on Jews, gypsies, Negroes and others as inferior races enabled the National Socialists to get other Germans to acquiesce in brutalities against which they might otherwise have revolted. It destroyed the framework of common humanity within which political policies had previously been debated.

Chapter 2

THE CONCEPT ATTACKED

Right from the outset many biologists and philosophers were sceptical about claims that the human species was naturally divided into races. Assertions that Negroes were naturally inferior attracted sharp criticism. In 1748 Montesquieu poured sarcasm on the arguments used in defence of slavery which he represented as protesting that Negroes were black, had flat noses, preferred glass necklaces to the gold that Europeans prized and *therefore* 'it is impossible for us to suppose these creatures to be men, because, allowing them to be men, a suspicion would follow that we ourselves are not Christians'. When, in the nineteenth century, the first formulations were heard of the thesis that race determines the culture of peoples, many of the leading intellectuals like Thomas Macaulay and Alexis de Tocqueville condemned the poor reasoning on which they relied. John Stuart Mill, for example, thundered in 1848, 'of all the vulgar modes of escaping from the consideration of the effect of social and moral influences on the human mind, the most vulgar is that of attributing the diversities of conduct and character to inherent natural differences'.

The critics won all the arguments, but yet as time went on they had to struggle all the harder. The racists often argued that though they could not yet prove that there was a hierarchy of races, much was still to be discovered and there was reason to expect that proof soon would be forthcoming. Because of the new political structures within the European countries, often related to the maintenance of colonial empires, there were many white people who wanted to believe in racial superiority. The critics demolished each new racist assertion, but they found themselves accepting that there were racial distinctions and that a racial classification of man's physical features, though not very rewarding, was not invalid. Physical anthropologists were committed to such classifications, and, while complaining about their misuse by popular writers, went on using them themselves in the hope that they could be made useful.

One of the most influential critics was Franz Boas of Columbia University. He studied the hair colour, height and weight, head length and breadth, and face breadth, in European-born Americans and their American-born children. In 1911 he reported important differences, particularly in the cephalic index (relation of the breadth of the head to its length, seen from above) which was a major technique used by contemporary anthropologists to assess the origins and distributions of peoples. Boas found that the round-headed East European Jewish children became more long-headed in the United States, whereas the long-headed South Italians became more short-headed. Both were approaching a uniform type. Moreover the influence of the American environment made itself felt with increasing intensity the longer the time elapsed between the arrival of the mother and the birth of her child. The significance of this finding was negative. 'I find myself unable to give an explanation of the phenomena' wrote the author. Though the changes were small they were in sharp conflict with the prevailing theory of permanent racial types and, because the changes arose within barely a single generation, it did not appear that they could be explained as the outcome of natural selection. Boas wrote, 'as long as we do not know the causes of the observed changes, we must speak of a plasticity (as opposed to permanence) of types'.

At first Boas maintained that 'when these features of the body change, the bodily and mental make up of the immigrants may change' but later he argued forcefully against the theory that race determined mental and social behaviour and showed why race, language and culture had to be distinguished from one another. Having undertaken specialised studies in both physical and social anthropology he was well able to show that ethnologists had not needed to give much attention to race because it bore no relation to the distribution of cultural patterns. In 1922 appeared the first of the classics of social anthropology, Bronislaw Malinowski's first book on the people of the Trobriand Islands. This, and some subsequent studies influenced by it, made little or no reference to race and yet they are important to our topic. Part of the heritage of Darwin's work was the idea that all societies could be arranged along a scale from the most primitive to the most evolved. It was assumed that societies at a certain degree of 'primitiveness' were roughly equally undeveloped in respect of all aspects of their culture: political, economic, religious, legal etc, and that behind this lay the undeveloped state of the people's minds. It was thought, for example, that primitive economies did not have money because the people could not evolve the principles of a monetary economy, not that—as we now know—the needs of a small-scale economy without the ability to store food-stuffs over a long period were better served by forms of exchange corresponding to ration tickets and licences in the modern economy. Malinowski showed that the Trobriand custom of tracing descent through women was indeed a custom and not a sign of primitiveness. Social anthropologists demonstrated that cultures based on simple technologies had to be understood as coherent ways of life. They undercut simple racial explanations by providing much better interpretations of the lives of what had been called savage races. It should be remembered also that this was the era in which the theories of Sigmund Freud were beginning to win attention. The intelligent public was becoming less inclined to see inheritance as the explanation of all kinds of human variation.

REVOLUTION IN BIOLOGY

The most effective attack on the prevailing use of 'race' did not come from direct criticism, but from an intellectual revolution within biology which produced a new set of ideas to put in place of those associated with race. Eighteenth- and nineteenth-century biology was characterised by what the eminent evolutionist Ernst Mayr has called 'typological thinking'. He likened it to the idealism of Plato and Aristotle, to whom variety in the world was as unreal as the different forms which the shadows of an object could cast on the wall of a cave. The philosophers' task was to find the pure form, the fixed idea, behind the various representations. The eighteenth-century Swedish botanist Linnaeus achieved fame by producing a classification of all known plants which extracted order from natural diversity. Scientists of his generation believed that by finding the categories to which animals, plants and objects belonged they were uncovering new sections of God's plan for the universe. Nineteenth-century race theorists inherited much of this way of looking at things. When a man died, his relatives wanted his body decently buried; the idea of giving it to an anatomist for dissection was distasteful. So the pioneers in this field had very few skulls and skeletons to work from and often failed to recognise how great was the variation within the categories they thought they had found. In botany the tendency had been to stress the true characteristics of each type and one famous biologist, Ernst Haeckel, who made a collection of deviant specimens that were not as they should be, kept it secret as something rather shocking. The features of individual specimens were not of great interest; they were seen as representations of a pure type and any questions about their nature were answered by reference to the place in the natural order to which their type belonged.

So was it to be with man. There appeared to be a diversity of forms possibly comparable with that of plants. Common observation showed that in many respects children resemble their parents. Skull shape, skin colour, hair type, appeared to be inherited. These were morphological traits, ie features of outward shape. They lent themselves to scientific measurement better than apparent variations in mental characters and seemed to be the obvious bases for developing a classification. No doubt the outward and visible signs would prove to be indicators of other less easily measured differences. Thus 'race' started its scientific career as a concept in comparative morphology, with an attendant stress upon pure types. When individuals were found who did not fit into the pattern, their characteristics were explained as the outcome of interbreeding of racial types and regarded as of only incidental interest. But comparative morphology did not prove the major line of advance in biology; with the publication of *The Origin of Species* and the subsequent rise of genetics, interest moved away from debate about pure forms towards processes of change and individual characteristics. Apparently deviant cases became of special interest. The 1930s saw the formulation of a theory of population genetics based on the work of two British scientists, the statistician R. A. Fisher and the biochemist J. B. S. Haldane, and the American geneticist Sewall Wright. It meant a transition from typological thinking to what Mayr has called 'populationist thinking', from the search for pure forms to the statistical analysis of variety. This change spelled the end for the old concept of race. To understand how it came about it is necessary to go back in time and consider something of what had happened in biology during the previous sixty years.

MENDEL UNTIES THE PACKAGE

A racial type was defined by a number of features which are supposed to go together. A Negro has curly hair, broad nose, thick lips and a brown skin. A Caucasian has straight hair, narrow nose, thin lips and a pink skin. The racial theorists of the nineteenth century assumed there was a natural law which said that such traits were invariably associated and were transmitted to the next generation as part of a package deal. Gregor Mendel's research showed that this was not necessarily the case. If all the people in one generation had one set of features, their children would have the same ones because there were no others for them to inherit. But if this seemingly uniform first generation were to mate with persons of a physically distinct population, then the next generation would contain many novel combinations of features. There would be a complex pattern of diversity that could be explained in terms of statistical laws. To represent it as the blending of two types was fundamentally misleading. Mendel's work also showed that trait variation *within* a population was just as significant as trait variations *between* populations. The concept of type obscured this by emphasising between-population variation and dismissing within-population variation.

In the 1860s Mendel performed carefully designed experiments with the common garden pea plant, noting the presence among parents and offspring of particular traits like plant height, shape of seed and colour of pod. He found that the inheritance of these traits occurred in a regular law-like way and suggested that the process was determined by particles which we now call genes. Mendel's laws have since been found to explain the inheritance of traits in all kinds of organisms including man.

Mendel's first law was that inheritance is particulate: it is the outcome of the association in the offspring of independent genes from each parent and not the blending of the parents' heredity to produce a mixed character, as many nineteenth-century biologists had believed. A corollary of this law—the concept of dominance—means that some of an individual's genes might not be expressed. For example, if one human parent is a Nigerian with brown eyes and the other English with blue eyes, all the children will almost certainly have brown eyes. The gene for brown eyes is dominant over that for blue eyes, which is recessive. This does not mean that the gene for brown eyes is stronger than the other one in the sense of extinguishing it. It only sends it underground. If a child of that union marries someone else with brown eyes who had a blue-eyed parent, blue eyes may reappear in the third generation. In the second generation both parents would have had one gene for brown and one for blue eyes although their own eyes would have been brown. In the third generation a child could inherit a blue-eye gene from each parent. He would have two blue-eye genes and his own eyes would be blue.

This example shows why it is important to distinguish an organism's genotype from its phenotype. These are two important terms which we shall be obliged to use constantly. The *genotype* is the underlying genetic constitution in respect of a particular trait or traits. The *phenotype* is the organism's actual visible or measurable appearance in respect of a trait or traits. The phenotype is what one sees: the appearance or behaviour of an organism. All people with brown eyes have the same phenotype in respect of eye colour. Yet some of them may carry a recessive gene for blue eyes and therefore have a different genotype. For predicting inheritance it is the genotype which is important.

Mendel's second law was that separate characters are independently inherited, that is to say that the inheritance of eye colour is independent of the inheritance of skin colour. We can see this law at work if we look at the diversity of human faces amongst any collection of people in a city bus or office. Some pink-skinned persons have tightly curled hair and thick lips and broad noses. Some have similar skin colour with straight hair or thin lips or narrow noses. These traits do not form part of a package but can be shuffled like a pack of playing cards.

Despite the importance of these principles, the vast majority of human traits cannot be explained by them alone. The peas Mendel used had either a smooth skin or a wrinkled skin because this characteristic is controlled by a single gene pair, one gene from each parent. The inheritance of eye colour is also relatively simple, though not quite as simple as we have suggested. Some people have eyes of intermediate colour suggesting that more genes may be involved. The inheritance of blood in groups A, B and O is also determined by a single gene pair drawing from among several known genes. But many other characters of the kind used in racial classifications are more complicated and less is known about their determinants. It is more difficult to study the inheritance of height, head shape and skin colour because these features do not fall simply into distinct phenotypic classes. They show continuous variation. If we make a graph to show how many people there are 5ft 6in, 5ft 7in, 5ft 8in, 5ft 9in tall and so on, we show the results as a smooth curve because there are people 5ft 7¼in, 5ft 7½in, 5ft 7¾in tall, and of heights in between those. There are no natural breaks in the scale. Characters like these depend on more than one gene pair. Theories about 'polygenic' inheritance have been formulated to deal with continuous variation and the absence of distinct phenotypic classes. Rarely do they suggest that each phenotype of a continuously varying character is determined by a separate gene because there are simply not enough genes in the human hereditary material to account for all the forms of diversity in such a way. The answer must be more complicated and non-genetic or 'environmental' factors must play a larger part than they do in the inheritance of eye colour.

The gene is a long chain-like molecule made up of different kinds of links. By their sequence the links in the chain connect up like the letters of the alphabet and spell out 'words'. These 'words' are arranged in a 'sentence' which tells the cell how to make a particular cell constituent. Each of the 10 million cells in the human body contains an identical set of hereditary material. Each set consists of perhaps as many as 100,000 gene pairs. Since many of these gene pairs can exist in different versions, it can be assumed that, apart from identical twins, no two of the approximately 4,000 million humans on earth have exactly the same genetic make up.

The operation of genes in specifying the activity of the cells can be illustrated with reference to skin colour. The natural colour of human skin is decided by the amounts of three chemicals whose presence in skin cells is gene-determined. One is the dark-brown substance melanin, which is found in all humans but most of all in dark-skinned Negroes. Another is carotene, a yellowish substance which is found in the highest proportions among people in China and eastern Asia and does not show up very much among people with much melanin in their skin. The third is haemoglobin, a reddish pigment, which like the other two is found among all humans. Because Europeans have less melanin and carotene the haemoglobin shows up more in their colouring; its presence causes rosy cheeks and the ability to blush. (In the next chapter we shall refer again to haemoglobin when we summarise the results of research concerning the sickle cell gene, for this causes cells to manufacture an abnormal kind of haemoglobin.) One of the genes which determines the presence of melanin, is that for tyrosinase. When men or animals (such as rabbits) lack this gene, many of their body tissues will be colourless. This is the condition known as albinism. A human albino has a very fair skin, white hair and reddish-looking eyes with no melanin in them. Amongst dark-skinned peoples the occasional albino looks very strange indeed. He lacks just one gene, but because it affects all the cells of his skin he looks strikingly different.

It has often been remarked that when they are born, 'Negro' babies are quite pale-skinned. The melanin has not formed in any quantity. There are many biological changes that occur in the course of an individual's development from the fertilised egg through birth and maturation to senescence and death. This sequence of developmental changes is thought to be the result of appropriate genes being 'switched on and off' at specific times. Environmental factors are critical here because the presence of such non-genetic substances regulates which genetic sentences are read out at which times. For example even though human height is known to be controlled by genes, the state of an individual's nutrition at various times in his development can have a marked effect on the expression of those genes and thus on the individual's adult height. This provides us with an explanation for the observations about head form which puzzled Boas. His were measurements of phenotypes, subjected to varying influences, and inexplicable without far more knowledge than he possessed of both the underlying genotypes and the influence on development of environmental factors.

Hormone action illustrates how environmental stimuli can affect gene activity. An experience (such as excitement) is first interpreted by the brain, which instructs a particular gland to release its hormone. The hormone travels to its target cells and affects the expression of certain of their genes so that the cells' activities then change.* This means that two individuals of

---

* By the 'expression' of a gene, we mean the process whereby information en-coded in the gene is converted into actual chemical activity within the cell. This process is relatively responsive to 'environmental' factors, but it leaves the informational content of the gene unchanged.

identical genotype can display different phenotypes if they have been exposed to environments which bring out different genetic potentialities. The biological basis of behavioural traits like intelligence and personality is presumably related to the functioning of the brain and other parts of the nervous system. These are complex organs whose construction and operation must require a very large number of genes whose expression will similarly be affected by environmental factors.

The ever-present influence of environmental factors on the way genes operate means that both genes and environment are inextricably bound up in the development of every human trait. In the case of continuous variation, environmental factors are especially potent in moulding traits, as Boas found with the cephalic index. This, along with the wide variation in environmental factors, helps explain why continuous traits seem to show an infinite variety of phenotypes. This responsiveness to the environment makes genetic analysis very difficult and means that continuous traits are unsuitable as criteria for racial classification. The child of a marriage between a couple of similar appearance can still differ from them sufficiently for it to be assigned to a different category than that of its parents, if differences in continuous traits are used as criteria.

A second difficulty with classifications based on continuous forms of variation is that they result in overlapping classes. The classifier who plots on graphs the distributions of traits such as stature, skin colour and the characteristics of hair in different populations (as in Fig 1) often finds substantial regions of overlap between the curves. From Fig 1 the reader can see that individuals who are between 148 and 156cm tall could be Pygmies or Japanese, and those between 160 and 176cm could be either Japanese or Dinka. The arbitrary nature of race classifications based on a single continuous trait comparable with height may be seen in Fig 1 from the fact that the shortest Dinka are of 'typically Japanese' height (ie 160cm) and are closer to the most common *Pygmy* height than they are to the most common height in their own tribe. Any uniformity within such groups has far less to do with their members' anatomical characteristics than with the cultural beliefs and practices which their members share.

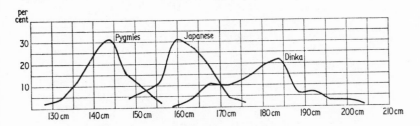

FIG 1   Distribution of stature in Pygmy, Japanese and Dinka (male) peoples (after Boyd, 1951)

For these reasons most of the genetic differences between human populations which have so far been studied do not involve visible anatomical traits. In Table 1 gene frequencies are presented for some of the genetically simpler traits upon which modern attempts at racial classification have been based. There are two chief generalisations that can be made on the basis of this information: (1) In many respects peoples of widely differing physical appearance have many less visible traits in common (this is particularly noticeable in Table 1B); (2) Peoples that have often been grouped together into one race on grounds of physical appearance turn out to be quite distinct in other genetic dimensions (in Table 1A compare English with Finns; in Table 1C compare Negro Americans with Baganda, and Japanese with Chinese). This should explain why no classificatory scheme yet devised has been able to group human populations into discrete categories without ignoring the sort of inconvenient information presented in Table 1.

Nevertheless, if we consider a large enough number of genes, it is apparent that conventional groups such as Africans, Europeans and Asians do have distinctive genetic *profiles*; that is, marked group differences exist in their overall pattern of gene frequencies as seen in Table 2. Because most of the genetic

TABLE 1

The Incidence of Various Genetically-characterised Traits
in World Populations

A Blood types:	*English*	*Finns*	*'Bantu'*	*Japanese*
	%	%	%	%
A	42	42	16	38
B	8	17	17	22
O	48	34	63	30
AB	1	7	3	10

B Blood types:	*Irish*	*Scots*	*Chinese*	*Finns*
	%	%	%	%
M	30	35	33	46
N	23	17	18	11
MN	47	48	49	43

C Colour blindness:	*Negro Americans*	*White Americans and Europeans*	*Japanese*	*Baganda (E Africa)*	*Turks*	*Chinese*
	%	%	%	%	%	%
	4	8	3	2	5	7

differences between these groups are not of the all-or-none kind,
however, it would still be impossible for us to predict precisely
from which group an individual came if all we knew about him
were his genotypes for the traits in Table 2. For example, if we
knew that he had blood types A and r, lacked adenylate kinase,
but had acid phosphatase, his probable group origin would be
European. There is a smaller probability that the man in our
example could be African and a very slight chance that he could
be Asian for we cannot be certain that blood of type r is completely absent throughout that continent. Such estimates can
deal only in probabilities. Similarly an examination of a baby's
blood can indicate that a particular man cannot have been its
father and that the father must have blood of a particular type,
but it cannot by itself definitely identify the father.

TABLE 2

Gene Frequencies for Various Traits in Conventionally
Defined Races

Trait	Africans %	Europeans %	Asians %
Blood types: A	18	28	18
B	12	5	17
O	72	65	63
R_0	75	4	6
R1	4	40	76
r	13	39	0
Xg	55	67	54
Enzymes:*			
phosphoglucomutase	22	24	26
adenylate kinase	5	0	0
acid phosphatase	17	36	22

From data presented by Bodmer & Cavalli-Sforza, 1970

* Enzymes are substances which facilitate chemical reactions in the bod·

Biologists interested in trying to formulate a better racial classification have sometimes maintained that when they had more information about the frequencies of particular genes in various populations all experts might finally agree on one racial classification. We argue that this is unlikely. Much more information about these frequencies has become available in recent years but scientists are no nearer to a comprehensive classification which contributes to the advance of knowledge. In its simplest terms the difficulty is that each individual and each population is genetically distinct and as there are no clear-cut biological indications of which differences are the most important, there are no biological grounds for deciding which individuals and which populations should go into the same category.

THERE ARE ONLY CLINES

The nineteenth-century racial theorists tended to think of races as fixed types of mankind which could be spread across the map of the world like fruits or vegetables, without changing character. They did not adapt to their new environments in any way that affected their essential, physical, nature. The theory of natural selection challenged this conception. It suggested that characteristics suited to the new environments would flourish, and unsuitable ones be eliminated. Moreover, it indicated that change would occur through individuals so that there would usually be as much diversity within races as other populations. It took scientists more than a generation to digest the implications of this revolution. The first experts in population genetics were generally more concerned to answer new questions than to rework the old ones for the benefit of a popular audience firmly accustomed to thinking in typological and morphological categories. But a few of these geneticists were among the biologists who prepared the 1951 UNESCO Statement on Race. This included the sentence: 'The concept of race is unanimously regarded by anthropologists as a classificatory device providing a zoological frame within which the various groups of mankind may be arranged and by means of which studies of evolutionary processes can be facilitated.' The claim of unanimity was dubious, for Ashley Montagu had for some years been arguing that the concept was not in fact fulfilling this purpose, and was more hindrance than help. The work of some geneticists had suggested a fundamentally different set of classificatory devices. An article by an anthropologist published in 1962 declared in the sharpest terms that the old racial classifications were worse than useless and that a new approach had established its superiority. This article, entitled 'On the Non-existence of Human Races', by Frank B. Livingstone, did not advance any new findings or concepts, but it brought out more dramatically than previous writers the sort of change that had occurred in scientific thinking. It is therefore convenient to use it as a springboard for explaining what that change had been.

The kernel of Livingstone's argument is contained in his phrase 'there are no races, there are only clines'. A cline is a gradient of change in a measurable genetic character. Skin colour provides an easily noticed example. As one moves from the northern parts of Europe, Asia and North America towards the equator, the overall trend is for native populations to have an increasingly dark skin. Plot this on a graph showing the presence of melanin and the curve, or cline, will rise steadily upwards as it moves towards the equator and down again afterwards. Similarly there are clines for characters that cannot be seen outwardly, like blood types. As one moves from West to East across Europe and Asia the frequency of the gene for blood of group B increases. In Spain less than 5 per cent of the population are of this blood group, in France more than 5, in Germany 10, western Russia 15, rising to 25 in central Asia and then falling off again. Such patterns may reflect the migration of members of a population away from their homeland, carrying their distinctive genes with them. Or they may indicate that by the process of natural selection individuals ill-adapted to the environment have been eliminated (with their genes) while the better adapted individuals (with their genes) have increased in number. Thus it has been claimed that genes for melanin manufacture are especially adaptive in the tropics because melanin protects the individual against the dangers of exposure to intense sunlight. If so, this will explain why human skin colour follows a similar geographical pattern to intense sunlight. The cline for skin colour may result from the gradual change in sunlight intensity.

Sometimes the cline for one gene shows a pattern similar to that for another, eg as skin colour gets darker, so may the percentage of people with black hair increase, and in these circumstances the variation is said to be concordant. When the clines do not harmonise, the variation is said to be discordant and it is then usually difficult to discern any types or races because the patterns are too complex. For example in any particular locality a person may observe a number of kinds of butterfly which appear to be quite distinct 'types'. But studies of butterflies on a worldwide basis have revealed that the various trait-combinations, so apparently stable and familiar to us as local observers, are often broken up, and the separate traits are to be found reshuffled in quite unfamiliar combinations in other regions. When we plot the resulting clines on a map, we find that because clinal variation is discordant, we cannot account for the unfamiliar kinds of butterfly in terms of the interbreeding of our well-known 'races' (or of any other primary 'types') of butterfly. Thus if we were to set up a 'racial classification' of butterflies, it would be an arbitrary one because while it would help the collector identify what he has in his net, it would not help the scientist explain the pattern of variation.

Much the same argument applies to humans. Classical racial theories of the nineteenth century tried to explain each population's particular combination of traits in terms of the interbreeding of a small number of primary racial types and consequent blending of those types' traits. According to this theory we ought to find that the clines in a given region for such traits as skin colour and nose shape or hair type and cephalic index vary concordantly; all the populations in the region would be, for example, descended from 'Caucasoid' and 'Negroid' racial types mixed in varying proportions. Much human clinal variation, however, turns out to be discordant, a fact which has seriously undermined the attempts of racial theories to explain patterns of human trait variation.

YESTERDAY'S SCIENCE

The modern attack upon the use of racial classification insists that variations in the human body and its behaviour are legitimate and often important objects of study but they must be examined in terms of particular clines and the mechanisms of genetic change. Racial classification is a hangover from an outdated phase of science which now does insidious harm. It has several times been observed that 'yesterday's science is today's common sense and tomorrow's nonsense'. Livingstone quotes this phrase, adding: 'For the concept of race and the intra-specific application of the Linnean system of classification, tomorrow is here.'

Science is continually formulating new and more precise concepts while allowing other old ones to be discarded. Usually it is not so much that a concept is wrong, but that a better one is found to replace it. The archives of science are littered with abandoned concepts. One such was 'phlogiston' a substance supposed by a late seventeenth-century chemist to be present in all materials and given off by burning. The existence of such a substance was generally accepted until our modern view of combustion was experimentally demonstrated by Lavoisier a hundred years later. Even so some distinguished scientists for a long time clung to what we would now regard as an unhelpful notion. 'Race', says Ashley Montagu, 'is the phlogiston of our time.'

We have tried to indicate why race was part of yesterday's science and have referred to the non-scientific factors which have resulted in its being part of today's commonsense. Yesterday's science was dominated by the philosophical principles of Aristotle according to which a scientist's first task was to determine the essential character of the thing he was studying. In physics the break with this tradition came with Galileo, who shifted the emphasis towards studying the movement of objects; away from explanations in terms of inherent causal forces, towards mathematical statements of interrelation and predictions of changes. Darwin's influence upon biology can be compared to Galileo's on physics. Before Darwin, the central concern of biologists was with taxonomy or classification. Linnaeus had brought order out of confusion by showing that everything could be classified as a member of a series of categories: first a genus, then a species, and then a variety (or, as it would now be called, a sub-species). This was, for its day, a magnificent achievement, but its significance was more limited than pre-Darwinian naturalists appreciated. The Linnaean classification, and subsequent developments of it including the racial one, were supposed to be more than descriptive. They were supposed to explain why things were as they were. The implicit explanation was that God had made them that way by elaborating progressively upon a simple original design. Thus a classification of genus and species showed a pattern of common descent like a genealogy in the early part of the Old Testament. So strong was the belief in the fixity of species and the static nature of the world that eighteenth-century writers believed it impossible for a species to die out. God would not have created it had there been no place for it. Consequently when men discovered the bones of mammoths and other extinct creatures it was held that others of this species must still be alive somewhere else!

A species is defined as a category of individuals who breed only among themselves. They are a genetically closed population and can evolve as such. If two individual creatures cannot interbreed (or, like horses and donkeys, produce only sterile offspring) they are of different species. There is no equally clear test for establishing sub-species (what Livingstone calls 'the intraspecific application of the Linnean system'). Indeed biologists seem to find the division of species into sub-species increasingly unhelpful because it does not aid them in solving the problems upon which they are engaged. As all human populations interbreed with alacrity there is no question but that man is one species; the notion of 'race' is a label for sub-species. To look at it this way is to emphasise what members of such a category have in common and to distract attention from what they share with others outside their category. Ashley Montagu, Livingstone and an increasing number of biologists insist that this is wrong because in many cases there are no sharp discontinuities in the clines and where such discontinuities are found, the patterns observed are rarely consistent with the notion of racial types. Racial classifications, they say, have no place in the advancement of modern science; therefore they are nonsense.

Chapter 3

RACE AND CULTURE

There never were any human races in the typological sense in which nineteenth-century writers thought of them. As we saw in Chapter 2, the human groups popularly identified as 'races' do differ in the frequencies of many of their genes but are in no sense genetically *discrete* (ie clearly bounded) groups. What makes such groups distinctive (in the sense of there being no overlap between their members' traits) is almost invariably their social and cultural characteristics. This means that anyone who writes about the social relations of groups should use not biological, but social labels, calling them nations, ethnic groups, classes, communities and so on. If any two groups in conflict, for example (and thus of particular interest to the social scientist), were to be exhaustively analysed by population geneticists, they would almost certainly prove to differ significantly in the frequency of one or more of their genes. As we shall see in Chapter 5, however, it is far from certain that the genetic differences between the groups would be at all relevant to the social relations between the groups. If it were possible to teach the man in the street this lesson by removing the word 'race' from the dictionary, it might be worth doing, but such a prospect is not worth the contemplation. If race relations are 'a problem' they will not be improved by making people change the words they use. If in some parts of the world racial tension is aggravated by the use of a typological conception of race, the proper response is to try to improve popular understanding of biological principles in order to show why this conception is inadequate.

If a pack of cards has been properly shuffled, they will be

dealt out in random sequence. When genes are dealt out to a new generation of babies there is the kind of diversity which, as we have seen, can be comprehended only by statistical analysis, but the sequence is not random. Every population, whether it be a nation, a local community or an intermarrying minority, inherits from its predecessors a collection of genes which geneticists call a gene pool. The next generation can draw upon this pool. Because there will be more genes of some kinds than others this will limit the ways in which the next generation can draw upon the pool. The frequency with which a particular gene occurs in the pool of one population will probably be different from that in which it occurs in the pool of some other group. Moreover, some characteristics are linked together and the clines for certain genes vary in a concordant fashion. Thus groups in different parts of the world look different. They also have different languages, religions and customs which were once thought to be part of the same package as their skin colour and outward appearance. When we refer to races we have in mind their geographically defined categories which are sometimes called 'geographical races', to indicate that while they have some distinctive biological characteristics they are not pure types.

This chapter explains some of the differences between the causes of physical variations and of cultural variations. Later we shall come back to this question from a different standpoint to show the reader how recent research has demonstrated that physical and cultural change are quite closely related, but not in the way that the racial theorists supposed.

Human evolution has been in progress for perhaps two million years. It involves two processes. The first is one of change in the nature of the biological organism; this results from the appearance of new genes, and then the operation of natural selection which kills off those organisms which are less well adapted to their environment. This process must have been especially important in the period of evolution leading up to the first appearance of *Homo sapiens*. The second process concerns social and cultural change, and because it proceeds on the basis created by physical change it may be called superorganic evolution. Its mechanisms are quite different; they depend upon man's ability to learn things after his organism has been shaped, and to transmit what he has learned to the next generation by teaching. This process, which is now well exemplified in the growth of libraries, has gathered ever greater speed during the past 100,000 years or so and has had a more obvious effect upon alterations in the human condition than any physical changes. Whereas organic evolution is the change over time in a population's gene pool, superorganic evolution is the change in its behavioural repertoire—that is, in the skills and habits the people have learned.

The problems of synthesising the very diverse evidence about superorganic evolution are forbidding. Relatively few anthropologists have been concerned with attempts to develop general theory in this area and there is no general agreement about its definition. Yet in an enterprise such as ours which relates the social and biological aspects of human grouping it may be valuable to try to express current understanding about cultural changes in terms comparable to those used in analysing biological changes. By superorganic evolution we understand those types of social and cultural change (usually entailing greater technological and social complexity) which are adaptive in the sense of making more productive use of the environment. This notion must be used with caution, for though it makes a useful contrast with biological ideas it runs into new difficulties. Cultural changes which are adaptive in the short term may prove maladaptive in the long term. Big cities are poorly adapted to their environments if we judge by their pollution problems. Their populations may have a high average income but the cities include appreciable sectors of poverty, of activities that can be considered unproductive or counter-productive, and of sharp conflicts. Seen from this angle, it becomes relevant to ask 'adaptive for whom?' but that is a question we cannot now pursue.

The organic changes which made culture possible were those responsible for the growth in the size of the human brain and the development of neural structures making possible thought, learning and language. Yet the examination of fossil remains suggests that these physical variations were stimulated by changes in the way of life of our distant ancestors who took to using tools and exploiting their environment in ways that gave a survival advantage to those individuals who possessed the most suitable anatomical features, thus speeding up the selective process. There was no sudden jump at a point in time when an organic change suddenly set superorganic evolution in motion. Man's organic potentialities could be developed only by co-operation with more and yet more of his kind, in effect by the establishment of society. Yet if men were to co-operate they had to suppress some of their own drives. They had to be able to calculate that small sacrifices could result in greater longer-term gains. The basis for co-operation lay in the formulation of rules of conduct and the first of these may well have been the prohibition of incest. Society becomes possible when a man does not mate with his daughter or sister, but allows her to rear children for another man who becomes his ally, and possibly allows him to take a woman from his own group. The definition of certain kinds of sexual relation as incestuous and the development of mechanisms to prevent them must have been one of the major steps in human evolution. It may well have entailed both biological and cultural change.

Since these early phases, superorganic evolution has probably been less dependent upon organic change. Nevertheless, natural selection continues and probably accounts for the variations in skin colour, hair and body structure which are thought of as racial. It is a much slower process than the artificial selection practised by the animal or plant breeder, and this is one of the reasons why it is so misleading to take the existence of races or breeds among dogs, cats, cows or sheep as a model for understanding the appearance of races among humans. If all dogs were allowed to run wild they would freely interbreed and the distinctive strains would soon be lost. Dog breeds have been produced by the control of breeding, first by geographical isolation and then by human planning. The animal breeder wants the greatest quantity and the best quality of meat, milk or wool and he controls mating until all the creatures in a particular herd or flock may resemble one another genetically as closely perhaps as do two human brothers. Man, by contrast, is a wild animal. No conscious agent controls his breeding so as to produce anything resembling the best meat, milk or wool. In earlier periods small societies may have been wiped out entirely by famine, flood or pestilence. Sometimes a few individuals will have survived though they will not necessarily have been so much fitter than those less fortunate. Possibly the brutalities to which black slaves were subjected when they were shipped from Africa to the New World may have had a selective effect. There are also less drastic processes of selection when men move to a new environment or modify the one they inhabit (as by felling the West African forests and allowing more disease-carrying mosquitos to breed, to anticipate an example we shall use later).

Natural selection in man can operate in either of two directions. The most obvious is that which results in the development of specialised abilities: a particular gene may confer resistance to a certain kind of disease or help the body to function at an extreme temperature. The other is that which results in what is called plasticity, a creature's ability to adapt itself. A species which can change its diet if its normal foodstuff is not available, or one which can change its habits if beset by a new predator, is at an advantage compared with one which has developed a highly specialised adaptation to a particular environment. In some species there is an association between altitude and the composition of the blood. They could adapt to living in a mountain range by specialisation, splitting into several sub-species each with the blood composition appropriate to its altitude; or by plasticity, in which case individuals' bodies would adjust the blood composition when they moved to a different level. Man's physical form shows many examples of specialisation but there are also many examples of plasticity which are too easily taken for granted. Some are physiological, like taking on a skin tan in different climates or losing or gaining muscle. Other forms of plasticity depend on psychological or cultural processes. Man inherits an ability to learn, to adjust to circumstances and to adopt different methods for solving his problems; his responses are infinitely more flexible than those of the ant or the monkey. Human societies all over the world value qualities of good judgement, patience and determination. Their problems are in important respects so similar that it is not surprising that their members should seem to share basically similar behavioural repertoires.

The main mistake of the early racial theorists was their failure to appreciate the difference between organic and superorganic evolution. They wished to explain all changes in biological terms. In our generation there is perhaps a tendency sometimes to think too much in terms of an opposition between the inheritance of specialised features and the action of the social environment, under-valuing all the ways in which heredity and environment interact. We shall return to this theme later, but at this point it is best to compare the two modes of evolution. We shall explain how the major geographical races are thought to have evolved from what was once, presumably, a single human stock with a gene pool containing sufficient variation to guarantee its daughter populations a wide range of evolutionary options.

MECHANISMS OF ORGANIC EVOLUTION

Genetic variation is produced by *mutation*. This is the process whereby an organism's hereditary material changes through a slight chemical alteration in one of its genes. Mutations are random events; that is, they arise in a spontaneous unpredictable way. They may be caused by an organism coming in contact with radiation of various kinds (eg cosmic rays, X-rays, radiation from radio-active materials used in the production of atomic energy etc) or with various chemicals. Mutations occur only very rarely, in a particular generation of newborn infants, perhaps only one in 10,000 or 100,000 would have a new mutation (relative to the parental generation) in a given gene. Mutation thus injects human beings with a continuous slow trickle of genetic variability which in turn provides human populations with the phenotypic variability that facilitates their survival in the face of changes in their environments. The recognition of mutations, shortly after the rediscovery of Mendel's work, undermined the typological concept of race because it rendered the existence of 'pure' types of race (in the sense of genetic homogeneity) extremely unlikely.

Possessed with the abilities to learn, remember and transmit his knowledge to others, early man must have had an enormous advantage over even the most advanced of other primates because he could develop and refine tools with which to modify his environment and make it more habitable, or to move to a new and better environment. Tool use allowed early man to fashion modes of transport and to overcome the physical limitations of his body: a man in a canoe is more likely to reach a distant island than the most ardent swimmer. Culture, therefore, facilitated the dispersal of early man by making migration easier.

The important consequences of this dispersal for the evolution of human races were twofold. First, imagine a coastal population in which the frequency of blood group genes is A—70 per cent, B—20 per cent and O—10 per cent. A small number of individuals from this population tire of mainland society and decide to pile into their canoe and found a new community on a distant island. They migrate, eventually reproduce, and after several generations a substantial island population exists. In view of the mainland population's gene frequencies for blood groups A, B and O, it would not be particularly surprising if *all* the original migrants to the island who had children there happened by chance to be blood group A. The eventual island population would therefore show a 100 per cent frequency of the gene for blood group A and it would have thereby diverged genetically from the mainland population. This is an example of a general phenomenon called genetic drift; it illustrates how chance can contribute to the formation of distinctive gene pools or 'raciation'.

The second important consequence of the migration of early man was that it brought human populations into different environments. These new environments varied in respect of climate (eg temperature, humidity) and the living world (eg food sources, predators, competitors for food or shelter, parasites). One of the best-documented cases of how natural selection can alter the frequency of a gene concerns the sickle cell trait.

For several decades it has been known that some black Americans and Africans suffer from a fatal blood disease called 'sickle cell anaemia'. The condition acquired its name because when the blood of a diseased person is examined under a microscope, many of the person's red blood cells have an unusual sickle-like shape. Such cells are often defective as oxygen transporters, and very few persons with the disease survive beyond childhood. In 1949 the biochemist Linus Pauling and some colleagues discovered that the haemoglobin ('Hb'—the red oxygen-binding pigment of red blood cells) in such people was chemically distinct from normal Hb and probably responsible for the sickling phenomenon. When the Hb from the apparently normal parents of sickle cell anaemics was investigated, the parents' red blood cells turned out to contain both normal (Hb A) and abnormal (Hb S) haemoglobin. The presence of Hb A, however, was enough to prevent the parents' red blood cells from sickling under most conditions so they showed no signs of anaemia.

Geneticists, familiar with the kind of inheritance pattern we described for eye-colour, suggested that sickle cell anaemia might follow Mendelian inheritance. The normal person's two copies of a gene for Hb would both specify Hb A (we can represent their Hb genotype as 'AA'). The anaemic's gene copies would both specify Hb S (genotype = 'SS'). The anaemic's phenotypically normal parents would have one copy specifying Hb A and one copy specifying Hb S (genotype = 'AS'). The evidence gathered from the family trees of sickle cell anaemics supported this hypothesis.

Because sickle cell anaemia was almost unheard of about 1950 among North Europeans, Japanese and American Indians, here was a simply inherited and apparently 'racial' trait. A method was devised for revealing which persons had genotype AS, and various investigators began to study the geographical distribution of the 'S gene' in Africa and elsewhere. They soon ran into several nasty problems. First, sub-Saharan African peoples varied widely in their frequency of the S gene. Central African peoples occasionally had frequencies as high as 20 per cent, but 'Negroid' populations in southern and north-eastern Africa had no measurable frequencies of the gene. In keeping with traditional racial explanations of trait variation, the earliest attempts to explain this distribution of gene S were based on postulated migrations of 'high S' races which interbred with 'low S' races in varying patterns. This explanation, in addition to proposing migrations that would at best be very awkward to verify historically, encountered further difficulties. Careful study showed that the S gene was not restricted to populations of known 'Negroid' descent but also occurred in parts of Greece, Sicily, southern Turkey, southern Saudi Arabia and southern India, sometimes at quite high frequencies. How was one to account for such an apparently 'non-racial' distribution? Furthermore these high frequencies appeared to be stable. Since sickle cell anaemics very rarely live long enough to reproduce, the frequency of gene S in such populations should have been decreasing each year.

A solution to the riddle was first proposed in 1954 by A. C. Allison who observed that the geographical distribution of gene S happens to correspond quite closely to the incidence of malaria* in the world. Allison guessed that perhaps gene S helped people resist death from malaria. People of SS genotype, of course, die anyway of anaemia, but perhaps the AS persons' Hb is just different enough from AA Hb not to be destroyed by the parasite. The AS genotype would then confer protection against death from malaria.

Such an explanation would be consistent with Darwin's theory of natural selection in humans. 'Normal' people (genotype AA) in certain geographical areas face a struggle for existence against a malarious environment. The occasional person might acquire just the right mutation in one of his gene

---

* Malaria is a frequently lethal disease in children caused by a microscopic parasite. The parasite is borne by the Anopheles mosquito and enters the human blood stream during the mosquito's bite. The parasite then consumes the red blood cells' Hb.

copies for Hb that would change his genotype from AA to AS. The Hb of his red blood cells would consequently be relatively resistant to malaria, and he would be more likely than the normal individual to live long enough to reproduce. About half the children of these AS persons would also have this resistance to malaria and would similarly leave more healthy descendants in subsequent generations because of the 'selective advantage' of genotype AS. Over many generations the proportion of AS individuals in the population would gradually increase until it reached the optimum level for that population's particular environment; ie when the disadvantages of gene S (deaths of SS persons from anaemia) began to nullify the advantage of gene S (superior resistance to malaria of AS persons over AA persons). These survival advantages would be most pronounced in environments where malaria is severest. Thus this population would have evolved (as measured by the increase in its frequency of gene S over time) in response to natural selection.

Over the last twenty years a variety of different kinds of evidence has supported Allison's hypothesis. For example AS children in malarious regions become infected in infancy by the parasite, but they are less apt to get a lethal dose of the disease than are AA children. It has also been shown that the wide variations in the frequency of gene S among central African peoples and elsewhere in the world correspond closely to the severity of malaria in the respective regions. Livingstone has also shown that the frequency of this trait in different West African populations fits with the pattern of migration and land use. As groups moved down from the interior to make more intensive use of the land near the coast, they cleared the forest. In so doing they created environments in which the mosquito could breed more readily. Malaria became more widespread and the sickle cell gene consequently became more advantageous. As malaria is brought under control by new methods the frequency of the gene is expected to decline.

This is apparently what has happened in black American populations. They have come from parts of Africa with high frequencies of gene S, but now live in a non-malarious area where this gene (in its AS configuration) confers no reproductive advantage, but is still a handicap (in its SS configuration) since sickle cell anaemia remains a life-threatening disease. The frequency of gene S among black Americans today is lower than among West Africans and is at a level consistent with a 300-year period during which selection has been reducing its frequency.

Although its connection with natural selection is the best understood, Hb S is not the only known Hb variant. By 1970 about 60 Hb variants had been discovered, some of them giving a relatively 'normal' phenotype like Hb A and many others giving a defective phenotype like Hb S. All of this naturally occurring variety in just one substance of the human body is an indication of the effects which the mutation process has had on human populations over several thousand generations. Some of these variants are undoubtedly of selective (or 'adaptive') value in one or more of the numerous existing environments in the world, and others will prove to be of adaptive value in future, as yet unanticipated, environments. (Note that evolutionists use the term 'environment' to denote a wide range of conditions. Dobzhansky, for example, has suggested the categories: *physical* (temperature, humidity, soil etc), *biotic* (other organisms as predators, prey or competitors), *social* (the situation with respect to other organisms of the same species), and *genetic* (how each new genotype whose adaptive value is being assessed fits in with the other existing genes of the organism in question).)

The sickle cell anaemia story shows that genetic variation *within* populations is more important than the racial theorists ever dreamed. Nor is it solely the outcome of migration and mixing. Trait variation between individuals is better seen as a population's protection against environmental changes and a resource which aids the population's survival. The story also shows that the adaptive value of a genotype must be assessed with reference to a particular environment. Gene S is selected *for* in malarious regions and selected *against* in others. Moreover, the story reminds us of the enormous importance of natural selection in the divergent evolution of early human populations in periods when their environmental circumstances differed very greatly. Selection is still at work. For example colour blindness occurs more frequently in modern industrial populations than amongst those which are dependent on hunting to obtain food. Parallel population differences in hearing and visual acuity have also been found. But with the invention of aids like spectacles and with the techniques of modern medicine, natural selection is no longer steering the evolution of human populations in the same directions as before.

Lastly the case of sickle cell anaemia suggests the enormous importance which disease is likely to have had as a selective agent moulding the evolution of human populations. One need only recall the catastrophic effects of bubonic plague which in the middle of the fourteenth century is thought to have killed one-third of the population of England and perhaps one-quarter of the entire European population. Smallpox, tuberculosis and cholera have in their day also been of significance.

Our current view, that evolutionary mechanisms are continually at work modifying populations' gene frequencies, has implications not only for the nineteenth-century attempts at race classification but for present-day attempts as well. Since populations' genetic compositions vary over time, race classifications can never be permanent; today's classification may be obsolete in 100 generations. More importantly, modern race classifications attempt to avoid being arbitrary by putting populations *of presumed common evolutionary descent* into the same racial group. Common descent, however, is inferred from similarity in gene frequencies, and here the problem lies. For, as we have seen, a population's gene frequencies are determined not only by its ancestry but also by the processes of natural selection and genetic drift. This means that two populations could, in principle, be historically unrelated but genetically quite similar if they had been independently subject to similar evolutionary forces. To place them in the same racial group would, as a step in the study of evolution, be quite misleading. In the absence of historical evidence of descent, therefore, it is difficult to avoid the conclusion that classifying races is merely a convenient but biologically arbitrary way of breaking down the variety of gene frequency data into a manageable number of categories.

These last observations will bring home to many readers how far we now are from what in the popular understanding seemed to be the certainties of Darwin's conclusions about the beneficent effects of natural selection. Darwin's work reached a wider audience through the popularity of some of the phrases associated with the social message which other writers derived from it. Darwin wrote about 'the struggle for existence'. This did not consist wholly of war, death, famine and competition between members of the same species. As the sickle cell example shows, much of the struggle was with the environment, and it was a question of gradual adaptation rather than sudden drama. The most popular catch-phrase was that which represented natural selection as 'the survival of the fittest'. It was coined by Herbert Spencer and used enthusiastically by the social Darwinists. They portrayed evolution as a constant struggle between individuals, who competed with others of their own species as well as with those individuals of other species. They ignored Darwin's evidence that co-operation is also important, for a species whose members help one another will be at an advantage compared with one in which there is no co-operation. The social Darwinists portrayed some people as fit and others as unfit, whereas our example has shown that one can only consider fitness relative to particular environments. Moreover they were easily led into circular reasoning. 'The fittest survive. We have survived therefore we are among the fittest. How do we know? Because we have survived.' There was no independent assessment of 'fitness'. To the biologist, fitness means simply reproductive efficiency. An individual or group which has more offspring than another is counted as the fitter. Darwin, indeed, spoke of 'sexual selection' when referring to the way particular kinds of individuals may be preferred as mating partners and therefore leave more descendants. According to this biological criterion, many of those whom social Darwinists regarded as paragons of human excellence were far from being fit!

REPRODUCTIVE ISOLATION

Genetic drift and natural selection acting on mutation's raw material serve to differentiate genetically human populations which inhabit different environments, but why has interbreeding of different populations not turned us into a more homogeneous species? The large geographic races (and to a lesser extent each identifiable human population) have remained reproductively isolated from one another—thus maintaining their statistical genetic differences—for two main reasons. One is the obvious fact of geographical isolation. Long distances and awkward geological barriers (oceans, mountain ranges, deserts) tend to prevent populations from interbreeding. Not surprisingly, therefore, most North Africans resemble one another more than they resemble sub-Saharan Africans (probably they are genetically more homogeneous, too). Similarly, Russians east and west of the Urals look different, and Europeans appear distinct from American Indians.

The other isolating factor is social or cultural in nature. Both within and between societies there are often barriers to intermarriage between individuals belonging to certain groups. Some tribal groups have marriage rules which severely restrict the number of girls from among whom a boy may choose a bride. In many European villages a young man has had little opportunity to meet girls from far away and the young men have often made it difficult for an outsider to court a girl belonging to 'their' village. A more extreme example is that rules proscribing intermarriage between Hindu castes have been enforced for over 2,000 years and have led to significant genetic differences between some castes.

Cultural and geographic factors thus maintain genetic differences between populations by discouraging outbreeding. If individuals cannot breed out, they breed in, and therefore retain particular combinations of genes intact over many generations. This process of divergent evolution of relatively isolated populations ('raciation') has presumably been in train for several tens of thousands of years at the same time as other processes have been bringing populations together and operating in a contrary direction. In the last 300 years there have been far more instances of mating between persons of African and European stock (notably in Brazil and the United States) than there were in the previous 300. There must therefore be more people who combine features (like curly hair and a pale skin) which were previously characteristic of the one population only.

The question of the relative fitness of these hybrids is important to the process of raciation. If they survive and reproduce more successfully than their parent populations the gap between the parent populations will be steadily reduced. If the hybrids are less fit, their proportion of the population in subsequent generations will decrease. This source of gene exchange between the two original populations will thus gradually dry up, and as a result the two populations will continue to evolve farther apart until they are completely isolated from each other in respect of reproduction. At this point they will have become separate species.

It is for this reason important to consider the rather scanty evidence on the fitness of the children of interracial matings. We know from animal and plant studies that such traits as body weight, life span, fertility, resistance to disease and other aspects of biological fitness are generally lower in inbred strains than in hybrid or 'mongrel' strains. For example, the development of hybrid corn strains on this principle has enormously increased farmers' yields and has been considered probably the greatest practical achievement of genetics. This improvement is known as 'hybrid vigour', but it is not always observed, and it would be dangerous to infer that it happens to any comparable extent in *Homo sapiens*. Some human biologists have concluded that there is no evidence for lower fertility in the offspring of miscegenation. Early in the twentieth century, Franz Boas presented evidence that 'half blood' American Indians were more 'fit' than full-blood Indians and similar conclusions have been drawn from studies of German and Italian children whose fathers were Negro Americans serving in the occupying armies after World War II, though the evidence is not very satisfactory.

But in view of the multitude of genetically different human populations in the world, it would be misleading to attempt a general answer to this question. It is safest to conclude that there is no genetic support either for the encouragement or the repression of intergroup gene exchange in man. It should also be recognised that children of mixed marriages often have to contend with discrimination if their appearance evokes the prejudice of others, but this is because they are regarded as socially marginal and is not caused by their biological inheritance.

Although cultural factors in some respects promote reproductive isolation in other ways they undermine it. Science and technology reduced geographical barriers to contact between distant populations. Arguably, too, the growth of worldwide communications systems which rely on a relatively small number of languages has reduced barriers to interbreeding. Only a century ago the likelihood of marrying someone of different nationality was very slight, even in Europe, except for members of the nobility. Lastly, man's capacity for culture (deriving from his brain structure) has equipped all human populations with a set of adaptive mechanisms essentially lacking in all other species. Rather than having to adapt to an environment through the laborious natural selective process of genetic specialisation and then being suited to no other, man's bag of cultural tricks allows him to adapt to new environments quickly without major genetic changes. As a result human races can occupy some of the most diverse environments throughout the world while remaining genetically quite similar, whereas races of non-cultural animal species inhabiting a comparable diversity of environments have to develop more extensive genetic specialisations.

Culture-capacity has meant that man in every population can transcend his physical limitations as an ordinary mammal by 'using his head'. As we shall see below, there is reason to believe that this common endowment has subjected all human populations to very similar selective pressures, thus fostering these populations' *parallel* and at times reticulate (see Chapter 5) rather than divergent organic evolution.

GENERAL AND SPECIFIC EVOLUTION

It is difficult to describe superorganic or socio-cultural evolution with the same precision as organic evolution. In the cultural realm there are so many variables at work. It is possible, for example, to consider the Bushmen of the Kalahari Desert in south-west Africa, and the Aborigines of north and central Australia, as examples of human populations which are less evolved than others. Such a procedure has its dangers. In the first place, peoples with relatively primitive economies living in harsh environments may have been pushed into these regions by stronger groups taking over the territory they previously inhabited. In the second place, these regions may offer no opportunity for their inhabitants to acquire the higher standard of living, the more highly differentiated culture or the more complex organisation characteristic of more evolved societies.

The full range of superorganic evolution has so far been evoked only in the more temperate latitudes in circumstances where there have been no serious obstacles to communication so that large political units have been able to develop. In these regions it is possible to rough out a very approximate chart showing how the population has evolved to its present state. This is an account of *specific evolution* and in its later phases it is a history of the peoples in question. If all the peoples of the world are classified, with the largest and most heterogeneous societies in the top category and the smallest and most homogeneous in the bottom, this produces a chart of *general evolution*. At the bottom come the societies where men and women live in bands, less than 100 strong; they get their living by hunting and by gathering readily available foodstuffs such as berries and root vegetables. A bit further up come tribal societies in which groups of several thousand are organised on a basis of common descent but without any chief or central authority. Some of these groups are pastoralists, making a living from herding cattle or deer. Above them come the simpler forms of state organisation with a chief or king who holds court and punishes offenders against law or custom. Many of these societies are agricultural. A further stage in the scale and complexity of organisation is that of the peasant society in which the power of the state is used to support a class of landlords who enjoy an economic, political and cultural position superior to that of the peasants. There will be many intermediate positions in such a classification but it can serve to indicate the stages of superorganic evolution, like a set of milestones, though the routes followed by different societies vary and there is no reason to expect them all to go through the same stages.

In the early phases of superorganic evolution organic and superorganic changes must have been interdependent. At this stage it is specific evolution which is the more interesting, even though we can only guess about how our ancestors may have moved from one spot to the next along the route. Several million years ago, it seems, some of them started to live more on the ground than in the trees, and then moved out of the forests to live in the savannahs, grouped in co-operating bands. Their way of life and their organic structure then started to change in a co-ordinated way. The key stimuli were the use of tools and the use of sounds for communication. Those ape-like ancestors who were able to use rough tools (eg a rock for smashing) would have been better equipped for hunting and fighting and would have enjoyed a survival advantage over their less imaginative brothers. Because tool-users who could walk on two legs part of the time had their 'hands' free more often, such partial 'bipeds' possessed a selective advantage as they could exploit tool-usage more effectively. As the 'man-ape' gradually became bipedal his hands, no longer required for locomotion, were free to evolve through natural selection away from supportive and branch-grasping functions in the direction of manual dexterity. Such dexterity gave these man-apes a further advantage in manipulating tools. Because the areas of the brain concerned with motor control of the thumb and hand are much larger in man than in the chimpanzee, it is likely that the reproductive advantage of our manually dextrous ancestors provided a selective pressure for gradual enlargement of these areas of the brain. This anatomical development in turn enlarged the scope of subsequent generations' cultural repertoire. Another organic development similarly prompted by the extension of man's cultural activities is that of the prolonged immaturity of the human infant compared to the ape infant. This period of dependency was presumably of selective value in allowing for the greater transmission of adaptive behaviour from parent to child. The higher vulnerability of the young to predators would have been offset by the parents' rudimentary culture, such as the possession of weapons. Anatomical and cultural evolution therefore influenced each other: a slight extension of the cultural sphere gave the reproductive advantage to the animals who were anatomically better equipped for it; this advantage in turn extended the cultural sphere of the next generation, and so on.

Once the man-ape had spears for killing animals there was a prospect of large-scale hunting. Four-legged animals were an attractive source of meat. But to organise hunting parties effectively, communication was necessary. At this stage those ancestors who were genetically able to emit a few systematically differentiated sounds would have had an advantage in hunting. We know that apes possess mouths and larynxes adequate for speech, but they lack the necessary brain structures to be able to use them fully. Thus the hunting successes of those who first used crude sounds to communicate may have rapidly constituted a selective pressure favouring the growth and differentiation of those brain regions and other anatomical features relevant to speech. Such a growth would permit subsequent generations to make increasingly elaborate use of language.

Language enormously facilitated hunting, but would not by itself have been quite sufficient. Co-operation between individuals (an advance in 'social' behaviour?) would also have been necessary for the success of this and other forms of organisation. Such organisation would greatly have enhanced the participating individuals' chances of surviving to reproductive age. Co-operation at this level demanded that individual instinctive behaviours (eg aggressive and sexual drives) become subject to self-control. Without such drive-inhibition the survival advantages of organisation would have rapidly been lost through the socially disruptive effects of giving weapons to aggressive or jealous individuals. Behaviour had to become more malleable and responsive to learning. Such learning would have been made easier in a species which possessed brain structures not only for language but for memory and reasoning as well. The adaptive value of drive-inhibition, similarly, constituted a selective pressure for the development of brain structures which conferred the capacity for guilt which could then be culturally programmed as the group saw fit. Rigidly patterned instincts or behavioural 'specialisation' are adaptive only in a limited range of environments and become a handicap should the environment change. Man's growing tendency to change his own environments through invention and/or migration made genotypes for educability and behavioural 'plasticity' a great advantage in successfully exploiting the widest possible range of environments. Modern corporations try to diversify their productive activities in order not to become too dependent on a single, fallible market. Analogously early man evolved broad behavioural plasticity based on the ability to learn from and adapt to all experience which effectively maximised his evolutionary options. Becoming over specialised in his adaptation to a single environment would have invited extinction, the fate of an estimated 99 per cent of all the species which have evolved to date.

This educability or knack of adapting to any environment (be it physical, biotic or social) is one definition of intelligence in the broadest sense. It seems reasonable to believe that in the course of his evolution man has always inhabited environments where this intelligence will have fostered his survival. Therefore natural selection will have favoured its development. Since all human populations are generally regarded as descendants of one original human stock, all geographic races will have been heir to this human legacy of behavioural plasticity and intelligence. Geographic races of man have, of course, occupied somewhat different kinds of environments (at least in climatic and biotic respects) during raciation over the last 100,000 years or so. It is conceivable, as several geneticists have indicated, that these environments were sufficiently different for the various races to have experienced slightly different selective forces favouring slightly different aspects of intelligence. Random genetic drift could also have caused some divergence between the intelligence of different populations. If so, modern 'culture-fair' tests would show various racial groups to possess somewhat different patterns of intellectual skill. Broad consensus does not exist on this issue, but most experts seem to agree that if there are any such racial differences they cannot be other than small relative to the range of ability *within* 'racial' groups. The question of detecting such small genetic differences between racial groups raises a serious problem. In occupying different environments over the last 50,000 years, these racial groups have developed very different cultural techniques for adapting to these environments. Therefore they respond in different ways to the problems posed in the psychologists' intelligence tests and it becomes very difficult indeed to separate the cultural from the genetic contributions to the test results.

Nevertheless there are some authors who believe that on these *a priori* grounds, and taking account of the existence of various fossil data, it is plausible to regard certain races as being further evolved than others. Our criticism of this typological approach suggests that this conception of race is suspect and profitless, but it may be as well to pause at the question of whether the *anatomical* evidence is sufficient to sustain this kind of claim.

The American physical anthropologist Carlton Coon has described the Australian Aborigines as both culturally and physically the most archaic of living human peoples. He considers them physically primitive on account of their heavy brow ridges, large teeth and only moderate-sized brains. On the basis of the fossil evidence Coon also believes Negro people to have '. . . started on the same evolutionary level as [Caucasoids, Mongoloids and "Australoids"] . . . and then stood still for a half million years . . .'

Implicit in the term 'further evolved' is the assumption that evolution is a *directional* process along a single path; *Homo sapiens* is evolving away from one condition and towards another higher one. Partly because the fossil history of some species does provide evidence of progressive change between one form and its successor, the idea of evolutionary change as improvement and progress towards perfection was prominent in much nineteenth-century evolutionary thought, including Darwin's. Modern evolutionists, however, are very much divided on this issue. Some are plainly critical of the assumption of progress and hesitate about making the value judgement necessary in proposing that one organism is 'further evolved' than another. They are more apt to be interested in the processes by which a population adapts to its environment. In this aspect, *every* organism so adapted is seen as highly evolved, the worm as well as the ape. Nevertheless if we provisionally apply Coon's rationale to human evolution, we might argue that the degree of evolutionary advancement of a skeleton can be assessed by the extent to which it differs from the ancient fossil skeletons of early man-apes. With non-skeletal features we might estimate evolutionary advancement by comparison with modern ape features. If we accept the limitations of these methods, a variety of other observations may be made about the evolutionary status of modern races which conflict with Coon's and indicate that even on his assumptions it is impossible to arrange them in a clear evolutionary sequence. To take skeletal features first, the pronounced concavity of the spine in the lower back region of Negro Africans makes them the *least* ape-like of human groups. Judging by jaw protrusion, Europeans are the most advanced group, whereas in respect of brow ridges, Negroes and Asians are said to be furthest developed. In the form of the chin, Europeans are more advanced than Negroes.

In the matter of brain size (estimated in fossils from cranial volume), it is still unclear whether the claims that Negro Americans have slightly smaller average brain volumes (by 5 per cent at most) than American whites are statistically justified. Some writers have stressed the evolutionary importance such a difference would have in view of the general belief that the transition from ape to man was marked by a several-fold increase in brain volume. While there is a rough proportionality between

82

brain size and, say, memory in various animal species, the correlation in living primates (including man) is far from perfect. Gorillas have considerably larger brains than chimpanzees, but are not considered more intelligent. Anatole France had a brain volume of only 1,017cc compared to the average for *Homo sapiens* of about 1,350cc. On the other hand Eskimos have been attributed with an average brain capacity of 1,563cc and the fossil La Chapelle man had 1,620cc! There are simply too many other factors—structural as well as experiential—which are likely to affect brain function, for small differences in brain volume to be of any value in predicting the intellectual capacity of contemporary men.

It is also of interest to note that in lip thickness it is the Europeans who most closely resemble the apes. Negroes and Australian Aborigines resemble apes in respect of skin colour more than do other populations, but as apes have fine, straight and abundant body hair, it is the Europeans which come closest to them on this score. It is difficult to see how comparisons pointing in so many different directions can lead to statements about the relative evolutionary advancement of the various races.

THE MECHANISMS OF SUPERORGANIC EVOLUTION

With the appearance of *Homo sapiens* and the establishment of human societies it becomes profitable to pay more attention to general evolution and consider the ways in which different features of societies similar in size and complexity are interrelated. For some purposes it is sufficient to lump together many different kinds of change and call them all socio-cultural or superorganic, but to explain why change occurs, does not occur, or takes a particular direction, it is often necessary to separate them. In the sphere of social evolution we include political and economic institutions, the organisation of family life and so on. In the sphere of culture comes both the material basis of social life and the way in which people organise their ideas about it. Sometimes their different aspects of life are so interdependent that the society is in equilibrium and the culture is static. Evolutionary change can then occur only by breaking into the circle at some point.

A society which, in the 1930s, was closer to equilibrium than most, was that of the Nuer, a cattle-keeping people numbering about 250,000 spread out over a large and relatively barren area of the southern Sudan. During the dry season they lived in villages composed of a few families and their herds of cattle. In the wet season they split up and moved to cattle camps where they had different neighbours. For most of the necessities of life the people were so dependent upon the cattle that E. E. Evans-Pritchard said they could almost be described as parasites of the cattle. This intimate relationship profoundly influenced the Nuer outlook. They had no chief or persons holding political office. The people were organised in independent clans and lineages which reflected the structure of the cattle herds. An important man was known as a 'bull'. A man was not supposed to milk a cow so each human household had to include a woman who corresponded in a sense to a cow. A young boy had his personal ox. If he was to marry he was dependent on his father's and father's brother's herds for contributions of cattle to be paid to the family of the prospective bride. Without sacrificing or giving away cattle none of the important ceremonies of Nuer life could be completed. Cattle were never sold or killed for food. They could only be sacrificed and then their flesh was eaten with unceremonious enjoyment. At many points of Nuer custom and religion there was a parallel in the realm of the cattle. Each family group had to be independent to follow its own herd so that there was no need for any chief to co-ordinate the activities of the whole society. Disputes were settled between the groups concerned.

The material standard of living of the Nuer was very low and on this account they would usually be labelled 'backward'. Their backwardness was not due to their race or their organic development. In one sense they were not backward at all, having progressed as far as their environment permitted; probably no other way of life would have enabled the same land to support the life of so many people. The limits to their super-organic evolution were those of restricted natural resources, and no innovation or change from within the society could take them much further forward. If their culture is compared with that of people who make a living by herding reindeer, catching fish or farming land, some interesting resemblances can be found. Reindeer herders often regard their animals much as the Nuer do theirs; fisherfolk lead a life which centres on fish and hold a view of the world which is influenced by the close study of fish; agriculturalists vest a special significance in the ownership of land, especially the ancestral land for it symbolises the owner's connection with his lineage. Thus the mental aspects of people's cultures often reveal an adaptation to a particular environment and it is unwise to classify these aspects as more or less evolved without regard to the way they help a group make as good a living as possible with the resources available to them.

Many environments have been capable of supporting more complex forms of social life once an innovation makes new developments possible. This is what must have happened when irrigation was introduced in the dry belt countries of North Africa across Mesopotamia into northern China. This is a region where heavy rains in one season are succeeded by drought in the remainder of the year. Agriculture depends upon preventing flooding and storing water. Once man had learned to do this he could move water from one place to another by aqueducts or canals and he could start to terrace the hillsides by constructing walls and trapping the water. The development of 'hydraulic' societies (as Karl A. Wittfogel has called them) has enabled the land to support much greater populations. If we compare countries before industrialisation we find that in the sixteenth century AD Holland had a population density of 95 persons per square mile (which was unusually dense for contemporary Europe) whereas in the first century BC the wheat and barley fields in Egypt probably maintained about 725 persons per square mile, while in the early twentieth century the population of the Chinese rice-growing province of Chekiang was 554 per square mile. The irrigated land produced a large food surplus which supported the first big cities and explains why it was these societies which launched civilisation and took the steps which made further technological advance possible.

Hydraulic societies made great new labour demands. The farmer had to put as much work into water control alone as the rainfall farmer in medieval Europe put into all his farm work. The great engineering works for water control demanded a labour force running into millions of people. To recruit and control them something more was needed than a local chief. Large-sized state organisations appeared headed by rulers with absolute power over the lives of their subjects; they presided over great bureaucracies consisting of officials who were supported from the earnings of the peasants. The officials kept records of food stores, rations, equipment, labour gangs, taxes and so on, and it is not surprising that it was their societies which developed the first forms of writing, improved methods of computation, and studied the heavens so as to make better calendars and be able to predict changes in rainfall and water levels. Disputes over water rights provoked hostilities with neighbouring states. The increasing demand for bigger armies and greater food supplies then led to the expansion of victorious hydraulic states into great empires. Such, in outline, is the argument that a technological innovation can lead to changes in many other features of a society and that its exploitation depends upon further social changes. In ancient times forests covered much of the Levant and parts of North Africa. Trees on the hillsides retained the soil and water until they were cut down by short-sighted cultivators. The rains then washed the hillsides bare and the cattle-keeping people moved in to complete the destruction of the environment. Once-great states crumbled under attack from without and dissension from within. The frontier of cultural evolution moved westwards to Greece, Rome and Spain, to societies which blossomed for a while before they came to the limits of their resources. For the first thousand years AD north-western Europe promised little development. The picture changed as this region increased its agricultural production by improved methods of ploughing and of rotating crops. Extra food production permitted the growth of towns but not to the extent of allowing the population to multiply and furnish a mass labour force. Having no reserve of labour the peoples of the region showed an unprecedented enthusiasm for power technology and the mechanisation of industrial processes.

In the sixteenth century this was manifested in extension of British and Dutch sea power and the dominant position the former acquired in the triangular trade of manufactured goods to West Africa, slaves to the West Indies, and sugar back to Britain. More and more of people's income was invested in the making of tools, machines, ships and durable goods like housing. If men were to ensure rapid growth of the economic system they needed a different outlook upon life from that which had been traditional. The Reformation and the Puritan movement probably played an important part in separating the sphere of business from that of religion, stimulating merchants to set fixed prices, to keep business accounts distinct from their household expenses, and ultimately to believe that everyone's interests were best served if each man sought his own advancement in a market place that guaranteed free competition. From the seventeenth to at least the early twentieth century, capitalism carried all before it, pulling more and more regions of the world into its system of relations. The course of superorganic evolution is now one in which the major innovations are made in only a few societies and are spread to the others by a process of diffusion. Change amongst the cattle-keeping Nuer has in recent decades been a process first of Arab traders penetrating the countryside, of Christian missions establishing schools and mission stations, of novel religious movements seeking to rally popular support on a new basis in opposition to the colonial power, and then of bloodshed as a newly independent regime attempted to establish its authority in the region. There is no opportunity for Nuer society to evolve further as a separate unit. It is caught up in international movements and its people have to find a place for themselves in a social system fashioned by the super-powers in terms of the laws which have governed their development.

Socio-cultural evolution in the contemporary world shows two contrasting tendencies. One is ever-greater uniformity based upon technological advance. The other is one of pressure to maintain diversity, and springs from political sources.

A striking example of the move towards uniformity is provided by language. Once Latin served as a fairly general vehicle of communication amongst the élite in western Europe. Then French became the language of diplomacy for another élite but over a wider geographical area. Now that the mass of people is participating more in world affairs those languages are favoured which, like English and Russian, are associated with technologies that bear upon the lives of ordinary people. Technological innovations now take hold with much greater rapidity than before. The first telephone exchange was opened in London in 1879. By 1932 there were eighty-seven telephones for every 1,000 Londoners. Compare this with the speed with which television has been adopted. In 1951 one English household in twenty possessed a set, but within ten years five out of every six could watch television in their own homes. Many programmes were watched by over a fifth of the total population. In 1973 over 500 million throughout the world watched on television the wedding of Princess Anne. Mass entertainment spreads uniform styles of speech and behaviour. Because of the costs of producing television programmes most countries show some programmes made elsewhere and in this way the language and culture of the biggest countries impinge on the smaller ones. Smaller minorities like the French Canadians or the Welsh find it increasingly difficult to preserve and cultivate their languages. If someone is to learn an additional language he chooses the one which will be of most use to him and these languages come to have higher prestige.

There are some factors which restrain the movement towards uniformity. The recent concern for the preservation of natural ecological systems stimulated by fears of pollution shows that a crude mechanical approach to living matter is a dangerous one. The British experts who wasted over £30 million on a post-war scheme for the mechanised cultivation of ground nuts in Tanzania did not prove as efficient as the African cultivators whose methods they despised. But the major force which counter-balances the technological emphasis is that of nationalism. The world that the super-powers have created is one of nations, as exemplified in the titles of the supreme councils: the League of Nations and the United Nations. The Nuer will have to find a place for themselves as members of a Sudanese nation. That nation will try to benefit from tensions between the Capitalist bloc, the Soviet bloc and the Chinese. Its government will seek to preserve a distinct identity so that it can summon the support of everyone within its boundaries for national struggles. The evolution of political institutions and sentiments of shared identity has to occur within a framework established by political and economic forces.

The balancing of forces for uniformity and the maintenance of diversity can be seen at work in situations of immigration. Those men and women who left their European countries in the nineteenth century to seek a better life in the United States were expected to become American citizens, to learn the English language and modify their customs to conform with United States law. But they were not expected to change their religion, for that was defined as belonging within their private lives. One result was that many Poles, Irish and Italians in the United States came to identify themselves as Catholics in opposition to Protestants and Jews. Religious identities became more important and cultural change in successive generations of their descendants shows the strength of tendencies which reinforce such distinctions. A society was created which expected citizens to belong in ethnic categories and black Americans have had to develop their institutions to fit this structure. A slightly different example is provided by Sikhs who have left the plains of the Punjab to earn a living in East Africa and Britain. Their religion requires the men to leave their hair uncut and fix a comb in it. Normally this is held together in a turban. In East Africa and Britain, where they are relatively small minorities, the turban has become more important to them, as a sign of their identity, than it ever was in India. All their desires to help one another and preserve their distinctiveness are summarised in their insistence on wearing nothing else on their heads. Such an assertion is understandable in the light of their social position and can be explained only in such terms. Thus some patterns of cultural change follow a logic which is independent both of organic evolution and of technological development.

Chapter 4

RACE AND INTELLIGENCE

If the concept of IQ had existed at that time, we may be sure that the nineteenth-century racial theorists would have declared that races could be ranked in a league table of intelligence. They were quite sure that some races had more brains than others, but they did not write about the positions of races on such a scale because they had no way of measuring intelligence. This is something of the greatest importance. It makes little sense to compare persons or groups for a trait unless we can measure it. All the talk nowadays about IQs concerns the performance of individuals in responding to particular tests. Whether individuals actually have a quantity of intelligence in the sort of way they have a quantity of hair is very doubtful. What the relation is between an IQ score and a person's 'real' intelligence we cannot tell. Probably it is a meaningless question because we cannot know much about intelligence apart from the ways in which we measure it. All we have are responses to tests, so that when people speak of intelligence it is essential to ask what measures they have in mind for these are the only facts in the case.

IQ TESTS

About the beginning of this century the Frenchmen Binet and Simon were asked by the Minister of Public Instruction in Paris to devise a test which could identify the children who would be likely to fail in school. By 1905 they had constructed the first 'intelligence test'. This and other early tests produced results that seemed to be valid and they were therefore rapidly brought into use. In the United States as early as 1913 scholarly reports were being published which compared the intelligence test performance of white and coloured children. During World War I the US Army used similar tests as part of the process of officer selection, discovering that Negro recruits scored significantly lower than white soldiers. The use of such tests expanded, though after the war they attracted sharp criticism. Much of the criticism concentrated on the difficulty of devising tests which were fair to people coming from different backgrounds. Many examples have been provided of questions which are very real to city children but unreal to country children or to very poor children. Otto Klineberg refers to one which required children to supply the missing word in an incomplete sentence. It read '. . . should prevail in churches and libraries'. The 'correct' answer was 'silence'. He remarks that any one who has visited a Negro church in the south of the United States knows that there silence is neither the rule nor the ideal. Nor are there many libraries in those parts. Other difficulties stem from the way that in other cultures people may not be motivated in the same way to answer test questions. Someone who tried using them with some Australian Aborigines found that they were accustomed to solving problems by discussion in groups and could not work well on their own. Klineberg tried a performance test with a group of North American Indians which depended on the speed with which the task was completed. The Indian children had grown up to do everything carefully and deliberately. They made few mistakes but were very slow. To have evaluated their intelligence on the basis of speed would have resulted in an unfair comparison.

Experts in the use of IQ tests are well aware of their limitations. H. J. Eysenck has written:

> Intelligence tests are not based on any very sound scientific principles, and there is not a great deal of agreement among experts regarding the nature of intelligence . . . The agreement between different well-established tests is usually reasonably close, but it is nevertheless far from perfect, and differences of ten points of IQ from one test to another are by no means rare.

However, some students of the question conclude that after allowing for such differences there are still certain overall patterns in test results which require explanation, especially when, as in the United States, all the children attend schools which show basic similarities and watch television programmes sent out on national networks. A concern with such patterns lay behind the long and technical article by Arthur Jensen entitled 'How Much Can We Boost IQ and Scholastic Achievement?' which in 1969 gave rise to vehement controversy. His views were echoed in England by H. J. Eysenck's book *Race, Intelligence and Education*. The issues Jensen raised have not been resolved to the satisfaction of biological and social scientists specialising in this field.

IS INTELLIGENCE INHERITED?

In Chapter 2 we learned that all traits have a genetic basis, so it should come as no surprise to hear that a great deal of evidence supports the conclusion that measured intelligence is to some extent inherited. IQ tests are normally constructed so that 100 represents an average score. Persons who score less than seventy-five are often counted as mentally retarded, and there is evidence to associate some types of retardation with the inheritance of particular genes. There is also evidence that people who are similar genetically tend to be similar in measured intelligence. For example, the IQs of identical twins are more similar on average than are the IQs of fraternal twins, and the latter are more similar than those of unrelated children brought up in the same foster family. As identical twins have the same genes, while fraternal twins share 50 per cent, and unrelated persons on average 0 per cent of their genes, this indicates that some proportion of the individual differences in IQ to be found in any population are attributable to genetic differences between individuals. No one really disputes this point. But we also know that behavioural differences between individuals are sometimes due solely to environmental factors; consider a pair of identical twins, split up in infancy and reared in different families.

More serious disagreement, therefore, exists regarding *what proportion* of individual differences in IQ is attributable to genetic differences between individuals and what proportion, to environmental differences.

In order to clarify what is meant by genetic differences and environmental differences contributing to IQ differences between persons, let us look at the results of an actual experiment. Through artificial breeding Cooper and Zubek selected 'bright' and 'dull' strains of laboratory rat on the basis of the animals' number of mistakes in running through a particular maze. Animals of the bright strain averaged about 115 errors versus 165 for the dull strain (Fig 2, reared in the 'normal' environment). Young rats of each strain were then reared *either* in bare cages designed to severely restrict the amount of sensory stimulation the rats received *or* in brightly decorated cages provided with toys etc. The two strains were then checked for maze-running 'intelligence'. In Fig 2 we see that despite their genetic differences, both strains performed equally poorly when reared in 'restricted' environments and almost equally well when reared in 'stimulating' environments. This pattern of results is of interest partly because it deals with animal 'intelligence' but more because it illustrates several general principles about the relationships between heredity, environment and phenotype. (We do not yet know whether this pattern applies to the effects of environment on the development of human IQ, but similar patterns have been found for the responses of genetically distinct strains of other organisms to a range of environments.) Fig 2 shows what kinds of behavioural phenotypes (maze-running skill) result when two different genotypes (the bright and dull strains) are reared in a variety of environments. What conclusions does this figure suggest?

   1.   Although all traits have a genetic basis, this does not mean that they are determined or 'fixed' by the genes. The genes we inherit merely specify the range of possible phenotypes which *could* develop. Which phenotypes *actually do* develop will then depend on the environments available for development. This means, however, that individual differences

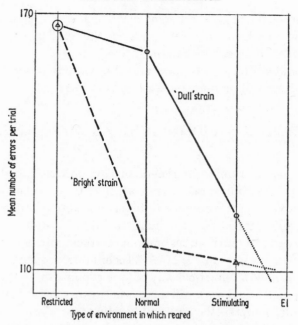

FIG 2   Maze-running ability of rats (after Cooper and Zubek, 1958)

between any two animals in respect of a given phenotype can be due to just genetic factors, just environmental factors, or both genetic and environmental factors. In Fig 2 this is reflected in the facts that (a) a bright and a dull rat will differ in phenotype when reared in a normal environment *purely for genetic reasons* while (b) a dull rat reared in a normal environment and a dull rat raised in a stimulating environment will differ in phenotype *purely for environmental reasons*. The phenotypes of a bright rat reared in a normal environment compared with a dull rat reared in a stimulating environment differ for both genetic and environmental reasons.

2.   We cannot conclude that the bright strain is generally superior at maze-running because we do not know what might happen if both strains were reared in a new, unknown environment such as E_1. Other experiments have shown that if such

strains are tested on a different maze or learning task from the one on which they were selected, the 'dull' strain may make even fewer errors than the 'bright' one.

The general significance of these two observations for the 'race and IQ' issue will become apparent as we continue.

HERITABILITY AND INDIVIDUAL DIFFERENCES IN IQ

If phenotypes can differ for genetic or environmental, or both genetic and environmental reasons, which of these explanations actually accounts for individual differences in IQ? If both genes and environment contribute to individual differences in IQ, do they make equal contributions or is one a rather more important source of variation than the other? Techniques of quantitative genetics provide a numerical way of apportioning this responsibility for individual trait differences between genetic and environmental sources—the heritability estimate.

A heritability estimate for a particular trait expresses the proportion of trait variation in a population which is attributable to genetic variation within that population.* If all the variation is due to genetic differences between individuals in the population, the heritability estimate is 1. If all the trait variation in the population is due to environmental differences between individuals, the heritability estimate is 0. On page 95 we have presented examples of these two possibilities—labelled (a) and (b)—in reference to the bright and dull rat strains. Notice from Fig 2 that the trait, maze-running skill, is clearly influenced in the rat by both genetic and environmental factors, yet the heritability for this trait can vary between 0 and 1 depending on the particular circumstances in which it is estimated. It is for this reason that heritability is said to be a characteristic not of traits *per se* but of *populations*.

* Another way of interpreting heritability estimates which may prove helpful in understanding these examples as well as others later in the chapter is this: as heritability estimates for a trait increase, the correlation between genotype and phenotype for that trait also increases.

Measuring the heritability of IQ in human populations requires conditions where we can hold either genetic or environmental variation constant and observe the effect of the other variable on IQ differences. One of the simplest methods used is to compare the IQs of identical twins which have been separated in infancy and reared in very different environments. The extent to which their IQs correlate is then a measure of how much *genetic* differences contribute to individual variation in IQ. Conversely we can compare the IQs of unrelated children which are reared in the same family environment. The correlation of their IQs is then a measure of how much *environmental* differences contribute to individual variation in IQ. The important point here is that while heritability estimates for IQ in human populations differ (depending on the particular populations studied), they are often greater than 0·5 (or 50 per cent). These heritability estimates indicate, therefore, that probably more than half of the variation in IQ within the populations tested is due to genetic differences between individuals, and the remainder would then be due to environmental differences between individuals.

Since the concept of heritability figures quite prominently in debates about IQ, it is important to clear up at the outset several common misconceptions about the meaning of heritability estimates:

1. The generality of heritability estimates is severely restricted by the conditions under which heritability is measured. Thus the only reputable estimates for the heritability of IQ we have up to now are based on IQ scores from a sample of the white populations in the US, Britain and Denmark, measured between approximately 1930 and 1960. Heritability estimates calculated for these samples are representative only of populations having similar environmental and genetic characteristics. There are various alternative methods of calculating heritability which yield different results even when applied to data on the same trait in the same population living in the same range of environments.

2. Remember that heritability estimates for IQ express the

average relative importance of genes and environment for persons' IQ *differences in a population* and *not* the relative importance of genes and environment in the *development of an individual's IQ*. (Because of the absolutely essential interaction between *both genes and environmental* factors in the development of every organism as we noted in Chapter 2, it is impossible to assess the relative importance of genetic and environmental factors to that process.) An estimate will *not* tell us accurately how important genetic differences are in accounting for the IQ difference between two particular persons picked out at random; for some pairs genetic differences will be quite important, and for others, relatively unimportant.

3. Similarly high heritability estimates (such as 0·8) do *not* mean that environmental factors can have little effect on an individual's phenotype, nor does the existence of large environmental effects in any way contradict a high heritability estimate. Consider height in human populations. The heritability of height has been estimated to be at least 0·8. The US-born children of Japanese immigrants to the US were on average substantially taller than their parents, presumably because of their better nutrition in the US than in Japan. But since most individual differences in height (in both parents' and children's generations) are due to genetic differences (ie heritability is 0·8), in general the children of the tallest immigrants would still turn out to be the tallest of the Japanese-American children, and the children of the shortest immigrants would be the shortest of the Japanese-American children. Height, like IQ, responds to environments, yet most individual *differences* in height are attributable to inherited differences between individuals.

Although Jensen believes that heritability for US populations may be as high as 0·8, he does not overlook the contribution of environmental factors:

All the reports I have found of especially large upward shifts in IQ which are explicitly associated with environmental factors have involved young children, usually under 6 years of age, whose initial social environment was deplorable . . . There can be no doubt that moving children from an extremely deprived environment to good average environmental circumstances can boost the IQ some 20 to 30 points and in certain extreme rare cases as much as 60 to 70 points.

Aspects of a child's environment thought to be relevant to IQ include cultural and social factors such as the 'cultural' amenities of the home, quality of education obtained at school, child-rearing practices etc. Aspects of the biological environment are also important. Jensen has assembled evidence that improved nutrition for the mother during pregnancy as well as for the child in its first few years after birth can increase the child's IQ by at least eight points. Unsatisfactory reproductive conditions (eg pregnancies at early ages, pregnancies in close succession, a large number of pregnancies) are also associated with lower IQs among the children so produced.

Now that we have introduced the concept of heritability and discussed its meaning for individual differences in IQ, we can ask what is the meaning of heritability estimates for *group* differences in IQ?

HERITABILITY AND GROUP DIFFERENCES IN IQ

Racially defined groups are not the only kinds of groups which differ on average in IQ. Studies in Britain and the US have shown that social classes or 'socio-economic status' (SES) groups (defined in terms of occupational prestige) also differ in average IQ. For example Burt's data from the London population indicate that persons in the 'higher professional' occupations had an average IQ of about 140 while those in the 'unskilled' category averaged about 85. All professionals do not have higher IQs than all unskilled workers, however; each occupational group's IQs span a wide range such that the groups overlap considerably. An American study found that the IQs of public relations men ran from 100 to 149 while lorry drivers had IQs between 50 and 149. How should we account for the higher average IQ of the public relations men? Answers to such questions are often classed as 'environmentalist' or 'hereditarian'. We have doubts about the advisability of using labels that encourage an over-simplified conception of the issues and use these only because they have been popularised by earlier commentators on the controversy. The environmentalist explanation for the correlation between IQ and SES emphasises the overlap in the two sets of scores and attributes the difference in the averages to the better diets, houses, schools, recreation facilities and other services available to children in more privileged neighbourhoods. Hereditarians explain the link between job and IQ in terms of social mobility. Educational and occupational 'screening systems' are seen as selecting people with intellectual ability so that high-IQ individuals rise and low-IQ individuals sink in the occupational system (and thus in SES). Furthermore because individual differences in IQ are seen to be due primarily to genetic rather than environmental factors, hereditarians conclude that it is very likely that SES groups differ in IQ on average primarily because of differences in their genetic endowment for IQ test performance.

POINTS OF CONTROVERSY

In the matter of race and IQ the basic observation, which has been repeatedly confirmed and is recognised by both environmentalists and hereditarians, is that on average the Afro-American population of the US scores 85 on IQ tests compared to the American white population's 100.* Because of the likely genetic uniqueness of all populations (as we noted in Chapter 2), the hereditarians have argued that the frequencies of various genes affecting brain structure and function probably differ among populations. Such genetic differences, it is thought, could well determine measurably different patterns of mental ability in the populations concerned. In accounting for the IQ gap, hereditarians do not deny the contributions of environmental factors. No one can overlook either the fact that US blacks are environmentally handicapped relative to the white population or that many of these environmental factors are likely to affect

* The average for southern Negroes is about 80 and for northern Negroes, about 90.

IQ. The hereditarians' point, however, is that even when one takes into account environmental differences between blacks and whites (such as SES), an IQ gap remains. Their evidence is as follows:

1. Reviewing forty-two studies in which Negroes and whites were matched in various ways for 'gross socio-economic level', Shuey calculated that the difference between average IQs for the two groups when all data were pooled is only reduced from about fifteen points to eleven points. (In these studies groups were compared which were similar in respect of such environmental factors as father's occupation, residential area and type of house, amount of education etc.)

Several studies have compared the IQs of black and white children who were matched for parents' occupational status and still found that the highest-status black children scored on average two to four points below the lowest-status white children.

2. So-called 'culture-fair' tests are IQ tests which have been developed in an attempt to compensate for the handicaps faced by the 'culturally deprived' child. These children usually come from ethnic sub-cultures which, often because of their colour and in some cases meagre grasp of the English language, are predominantly of low SES (eg Negroes, Puerto Ricans, Appalachian mountain whites, Mexican-Americans, American Indians). These tests have usually been trimmed of items which obviously favour the middle-class child by virtue of his differential exposure to particular kinds of knowledge. One kind of relatively culture-fair test is thus a 'non-verbal' test in which the child may be called upon to solve problems which concern patterns, figures, pictures etc and which require relatively little verbal facility. The point here is that while such culturally deprived minority children in general score higher on such culture-fair tests, Negroes score slightly lower on culture-fair and non-verbal tests than they do on conventional 'culture-bound' IQ tests. Although Oriental-Americans (ie of Chinese or Japanese descent) are generally not regarded as a culturally deprived minority, their average income is

somewhat lower than whites', they are at a linguistic disadvantage, and they encounter discrimination. Not surprisingly Oriental-Americans score higher on culture-fair tests
than on conventional IQ tests; significantly, however, their
average scores on culture-fair tests are higher than the
average scores of white Americans.

3. The Coleman Report, a nationwide study in the US
published in 1966, attempted to relate characteristics of home
and school environments to children's IQ and scholastic
achievement. Twelve indices of environmental 'quality' were
used, all of which were shown to correlate with scholastic
achievement and IQ within each ethnic group. Of all the
disadvantaged minority groups sampled, the lowest ranking
group by far on all twelve indices was the American Indian
group. Nevertheless American Indians on average performed
higher on tests of non-verbal and verbal intelligence and on
tests of scholastic achievement than did Negroes.

In light of these data the hereditarians conclude: (a) because
the black-white average IQ difference is about fifteen points,
(b) because in their view individual differences within the white
population are largely due to genetic factors (and it is thought
probable—though not yet established—that the same is true
within the black population), and (c) because attempts to equate
blacks and whites for environmental factors reduce the interracial IQ gap moderately but do not eliminate it; *therefore* (to
quote Jensen):

> . . . all we are left with are various lines of evidence, no one of which is
> definitive alone, but which, viewed all together, make it a not un-
> reasonable hypothesis that genetic factors are strongly implicated in
> the average Negro–white intelligence difference. The preponderance of
> the evidence is, in my opinion, less consistent with a strictly environ-
> mental hypothesis than with a genetic hypothesis, which, of course,
> does not exclude the influence of environment or its interaction with
> genetic factors.

Because of the extremely controversial nature of this issue, it is
very important to note what the hereditarians do not say. The
preceding quotation indicates that they do not conclude or regard

as *proven* that the IQ gap is genetic. They suggest that this is a likely possibility which ought to be researched further. Second, it is not claimed that the IQ gap is *exclusively* genetic. Nor is it claimed that entirely environmental explanations of the gap are *impossible*; such explanations are, however, regarded as much less *probable* than an explanation based on both environmental and genetic differences between the two populations. Third, *all* the American whites tested are not seen as genetically superior in IQ to *all* the black Americans tested. The IQ gap is based on averages for the black and white populations, and a wide range of IQs are to be found in each population such that the two populations 'overlap' substantially (see Fig 3) as we have seen is the case for SES groups. In fact 15 per cent of the black population have higher IQs than the white *average*. Conversely the number of US whites with IQs below the black *average* is larger than the *entire* number of blacks in the US. The economic, social and political significance of this overlap is considerable, as Jensen acknowledges:

> The important distinction between the *individual* and the *population* must always be kept clearly in mind in any discussion of racial differences in mental abilities or any other behavioral characteristics . . . The variables of social class, race, and national origin are correlated so imperfectly with . . . any behavioral characteristic, that these background factors are irrelevant as a basis for dealing with individuals—as students, as employees, as neighbours . . . All persons rightfully must be regarded on the basis of their individual qualities and merits, and all social, educational, and economic institutions must have built into them the mechanisms for insuring and maximizing the treatment of persons according to their individual behavior.

4. As might be expected judging from the quotation above, neither Jensen nor Eysenck view the genetic hypothesis—even if confirmed—as in any way favouring educational segregation by racial or other social group criteria.

It is also important to reiterate that Jensen's formulation of the genetic hypothesis is only valid for the specific (American) populations from which the data were drawn. Genetic differences in the average IQ of Europeans generally versus sub-Saharan

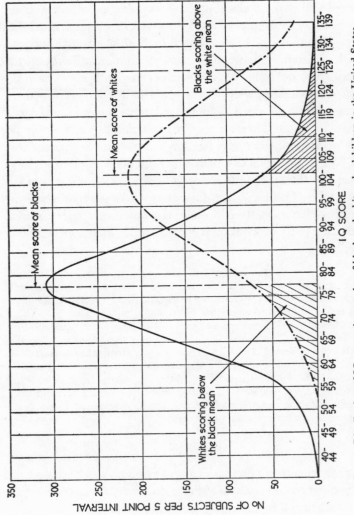

FIG 3   Distribution of IQ scores in samples of black and white schoolchildren in the United States
(after W. A. Kennedy, V. Van De Reit and J. C. White, 1963)

Africans are *not* being proposed, and so strictly speaking it would be wrong to call the fifteen point difference a racial gap. In addition, as Eysenck has observed, the real issue concerns IQ differences between groups defined in terms *other than racial ones.* For example he notes that the Irish perform substantially worse on IQ tests than the English. The various white ethnic groups in the US also differ among themselves by at least ten points in average IQ. In addition both black and white populations in the US are heterogeneous in respect of IQ along the SES dimension (as we have earlier noted) as well as along the *regional* dimension: northerners—both black and white—tend to score higher than southerners.

These interpretations have evoked a barrage of criticisms, some of them misplaced. In the following sections we assemble what seem to us to be the most cogent of the criticisms. These fall into three categories: (1) the significance of IQ, (2) the significance of environmental factors, and (3) the significance of heritability.

THE SIGNIFICANCE OF IQ

It is risky to assume that IQ tests measure exclusively intelligence in the technical sense of capacity for abstract reasoning and problem-solving. Many readers will know people whom they believe to be more 'bright' or less 'bright' than their test scores would suggest. American college students have to complete a veritable obstacle course of IQ and aptitude tests, and many of them would agree that there is a definite technique which can help bring success. The person tested should answer without puzzling long over any apparent ambiguities. Whether or not a student even notices these ambiguities may depend both upon his intellect and his personality. Indeed there is now evidence to indicate that personality variations can have a significant effect on IQ scores. We have already mentioned motivation. Although the data on this question are equivocal, even Audrey Shuey, a writer inclined to stress hereditarian explanations, has agreed that inferior motivation or 'depressed educational aspiration' cannot yet be ruled out as a partial explanation of the lower black IQ average. The finding that different kinds of mental test produce broadly similar results does not necessarily mean that *therefore* they are measuring a capacity for abstract reasoning.

Whatever IQ tests are measuring, we must ask, 'How well do they predict "success" in western societies?' IQ scores do correlate quite well with the number of years of education one completes and somewhat less well with eventual occupational status. Is high IQ then important for entering a high-status occupation? Not directly. Evidence suggests that while IQ is important for getting into and staying in educational institutions, high IQ itself (without educational qualifications) is of little help in entering a high-status occupation. High educational qualifications plus a modest IQ appears to be a good deal more important for this than few qualifications plus a high IQ.

Furthermore IQ scores do not correlate at all well with an individual's proficiency within his occupation. For example there is nearly as much income inequality among men with equal IQs as among men in general. Liam Hudson has brought together studies showing that 'men and women of the highest intellectual distinction are not differentiated from their less successful contemporaries by their mental test scores'. Similarly he finds only a poor correlation between schoolboys' IQs and their subsequent scholarship status or degree class at university. Furthermore IQ tests, because of their requirement that the child produce 'the' correct answer, give no indication of the child's capacity for imaginative or inventive use of intellect although these aspects of mental ability are clearly much in demand at several occupational levels. Although they are used widely in educational and occupational screening procedures, IQ tests fail to a considerable extent to detect abilities which are significant for both educational and occupational excellence.

Jensen has argued that in accounting for the underrepresentation of US blacks in high-status occupations, we must consider the possibility that this situation arises partly through the lower average IQ of the US black population. IQ, however, is a substantially poorer predictor of blacks' occupational 'success' than it is of whites' success. Studies have shown that whites acquire significantly higher status occupations than blacks of equal IQ. In addition the correlation for black adults between IQ and income in 1962–4 was practically non-existent; in 1964 blacks with IQs of 100 earned on average $4,300 compared to $6,077 for whites of equal IQ. As long as IQ continues to bear so little relation to blacks' economic disadvantages, an average IQ difference between the black and white populations remains of questionable significance.

It is important to remember what IQ tests are for. Their place —and it is a limited one—is in trying, rather crudely, to measure certain mental skills. They are not suitable as measures of all-round competence. Jensen writes:

> Before going overboard in deploring the fact that disadvantaged minority groups fail to clear many of the hurdles that are set up for certain jobs, we should determine whether the educational and mental test barriers that stand at the entrance to many of these employment opportunities are actually relevant.

The evidence is that IQ tests do *not* measure several mental abilities important in western societies while they do in all probability measure various individual characteristics other than abstract reasoning ability. Just what significance should be accorded the US black–white IQ gap—even if in some measure genetic—is therefore problematic.

THE SIGNIFICANCE OF ENVIRONMENTAL FACTORS

The black and white populations in the US differ in many environmental respects.* These differences undoubtedly go beyond the differences normally associated with SES. As a result, en-

* For example, the Negro infant mortality rate is approximately twice the white rate. In 1964 Negro men aged 25–34 earned about 55 per cent as much as white men of the same age. Negroes are also disadvantaged relative to whites in respect of (among other things) percentage unemployment, percentage of families where both parents are ordinarily present, and percentage of pregnancies and births which are trouble-free.

vironmentalists stress the need for studies which match blacks and whites not only for SES but for as wide a range of IQ-relevant variables as possible. Only when black and white samples are properly matched will it be possible to draw conclusions about the relative significance of heredity and environment.

As we saw on page 98, even the hereditarians acknowledge the large IQ shifts which environmental factors can cause. The evidence on this point can be briefly indicated. Studies of identical twins reared in different families in the US, the UK and Denmark found that the average IQ difference between twins was only about six to eight points. The range of IQ differences, however, ran from zero to twenty-two points. Although it is true that only a minority of the IQ differences were of fifteen points or more—the magnitude of the US black-white IQ gap—these findings suggest that group IQ differences *could* be accounted for by purely environmental factors. In speculating about the nature of those factors which account for the IQ differences between such twins, researchers tried to determine which features of these environments were accounting for twin differences. When they rated each identical twin pair for the degree of *difference* in the educational advantages enjoyed by each half of the twin pair, they found that the size of this difference correlated very closely with the size of the IQ difference between halves of that twin pair. Somewhat smaller correlations were found between the size of the twins' difference in social and physical advantages and the size of their IQ difference. Since even families of equivalent SES can provide quite different IQ-relevant environments for their children, these correlations illustrate the importance of classifying environments along more refined dimensions than the rather crude one of SES. These correlations also suggest that had the identical twins in such studies been placed in homes with *totally uncorrelated environments* (in respect of educational, social and physical advantages), more of the IQ differences would have fallen into the 'fifteen plus' range. In matching black and white groups adequately for IQ-relevant environmental factors, therefore, a necessary first step would be to assess home and school environments for the kinds of advantages described here.

THE SIGNIFICANCE OF HERITABILITY

A discussion of the heritability of IQ *within* populations takes up a substantial part of most hereditarians' arguments regarding the racial IQ gap. At this point we must query the actual relationship between heritability and *interpopulation* IQ differences.

Population geneticists have taken pains to point out that there is *no logical* connection between the heritability of a trait *within* each of two populations and the possibility of a genetic component in the average trait difference *between* the populations. In other words even if the heritability of IQ within the American black and white populations were as high as 1, this would not mean that the IQ gap between blacks and whites must be even slightly genetically based. Conversely the heritability of IQ in each population could be zero while the black-white IQ gap was entirely genetic.

It has since become clear, however, that genetically sophisticated proponents of the hereditarian position do not postulate such a *logical* relationship. Instead Jensen, for example, has argued that the higher the heritability of a trait within the populations being compared, the higher the likelihood that the interpopulational difference is in part genetic. Heritability estimates for IQ as high as 0·8, he argues, make it quite likely that the IQ gap is in part genetic. Even this more tentative probabilistic argument, however, has been criticised by several geneticists. Were Jensen's view to be accepted, it still could not at present be used because the information necessary for calculating probabilities is simply not available. (For one thing we have as yet no reliable estimates for the heritability of IQ in the US black population.) Consequently the significance for the black-white IQ gap of a high heritability estimate for IQ in the white population remains questionable.

Since available heritability estimates for IQ only express the relative importance of environmental factors for IQ differences *within the white population*, any significance which heritability estimates may have for the IQ gap will remain doubtful until hereditarians can prove that the main environmental differences *between* the races are the same ones which have been shown to contribute to IQ variation *within the white population*. If this were known to be so, the hereditarians could then argue that heritability estimates as high as 0·8 mean that environmental factors do not affect IQ strongly enough to account for the entire IQ gap. As we will see in the next section, however, arguments relying on heritability estimates could be overthrown if it were established that simply being defined as Negro is *itself* an intellectual handicap on account of the discrimination which black-skinned persons encounter in American society.

HEREDITY AND ENVIRONMENT—AN ASSESSMENT

There is no doubt that environmental factors can account for individual IQ differences of twenty to thirty points, an effect substantially larger than the average black-white IQ gap of ten to twenty points. Nor is there any doubt that US blacks and whites differ in several IQ-relevant environmental respects. The question remains, however, whether blacks and whites differ enough in known environmental respects so that these environmental factors are in fact solely responsible for the IQ gap. The conventional genetic technique for answering this question directly would be to compare the average IQs of Negro and white groups which have been carefully matched for all IQ-relevant environmental factors.* If a significant IQ difference still remains, the hereditarian hypothesis would be correct. If the gap disappears, the environmentalist hypothesis would be correct.

The matter is, however, not quite that simple. The problem with purely environmentalist explanations is that they are as yet still quite unrefined. Psychologists and sociologists know that certain environments have a marked effect on the development of IQ, but the detailed analysis of these environments in terms of *specific, causal* factors has yet to be achieved. This is important

---

* The need for this careful matching plus the impossibility of constructing a truly 'culture-*free*' IQ test explains why comparisons between US blacks and whites are methodologically preferable to those between modern Europeans and Africans.

because as Jensen has observed, '. . . the more fine-grained the environmental and interpersonal analysis, the greater is the amount of the [variation in] children's ability that can be accounted for'. But until the most relevant environmental influences have been identified and measured, black and white groups cannot be satisfactorily matched for them. This is a daunting task. Consider, for example, Jensen's comparison of the average IQs of American Indians and Negroes. Environmentalist critics have challenged his comparison by arguing that though both groups are coloured and disadvantaged minorities with low SES in the US, they are still not fundamentally comparable because Negroes are unique among American minorities in having a recent history of degradation through enslavement. Besides having been systematically deprived by plantation owners of their West African cultural traditions (including religion, language and family structures), slaves were classed in the laws of Southern states with farm animals, and their cultural history may constitute a brake upon the development of black Americans' mental and other abilities. By contrast, the Indians' organised defence of their homelands evoked fear and respect from the European invaders, so that one can detect a note of pride in the way some Americans refer to their Indian ancestry. As long as the specific elements in such a cultural experience remain undiscovered and their pyschological consequences for the individual undefined, however, it will remain technically impossible to equate US blacks with whites (or American Indians) in *every* environmental respect that may be relevant to IQ.

These difficulties in matching groups pose problems for the scientific status of the hereditarian and environmentalist hypotheses. For if the direct inference of a genetic difference between two populations requires environmental comparability, the hereditarian hypothesis can never be confirmed nor can environmentalist hypotheses as a class be refuted. This is because one can never be certain whether the two populations are adequately matched for relevant environmental variables.* It

* There are at least two ways out of this stalemate. It may prove possible

would appear, therefore, that the race-IQ issue is currently unresolved and that a decisive answer to the question may not be available for some time.

Under the circumstances it is very tempting to explain individuals' advocacy of the hereditarian or environmentalist positions at present as largely a matter of faith. Hereditarians are inclined to believe that American blacks and whites differ basically only on those environmental indices which have already been shown to affect IQ *within* either or both of the populations concerned. Consequently they regard the matching of black and white groups for crude environmental indices such as SES as adequate. When an IQ gap between such matched groups remains, they are therefore prepared to believe the gap is due to genetic differences between the groups rather than to as yet uncharacterised environmental factors. Environmentalists are inclined to think that subtle but important environmental factors (such as the effects of racism on Negroes' intellectual development) remain to be discovered. Advocacy of either position requires faith because at the moment there is no way to assess the likelihood that unknown IQ-relevant environmental differences between black and white exist. Comparability has also been disputed in those few studies where matched black and white samples have not differed in average IQ. Hereditarians have objected that in matching the two samples for environmental variables, the researchers ended up comparing blacks of above average genetic endowment for IQ with whites of below average endowment. Again there are at the moment no means of assessing whether the black or white samples studied so far are genetically representative of their respective populations in order to evaluate the hereditarians' objection.

---

quite soon to show that equating black and white populations for just a few more environmental variables than are currently measurable, will be sufficient to eliminate the IQ gap; that is, a *specific* environmentalist hypothesis could be confirmed. In addition Jensen has suggested several indirect approaches to the problem, some of which at least avoid the issue of comparability, but the development of the necessary techniques would require further research.

We have tried to avoid discussing the issues in terms of faith and to keep to the evaluation of the evidence. In presenting the ways that others interpret this evidence we have referred to two positions which are commonly called hereditarian and environmentalist. We did so because readers will readily recognise these opposed points of view, but we do not wish to encourage the idea that there are only two alternative standpoints with an unbridgeable gulf between them. Readers will have noticed that hereditarians like Jensen and Eysenck allow a significant place to environmental factors and are much less extreme in their views than some of their scientifically illiterate supporters. Nearly all the research workers who believe the black-white IQ gap to be environmental also acknowledge that the capacity measured by IQ tests is to some extent inherited. There is one controversy about the relative importance of genetic variation *within* populations and another, much bigger one, about differences *between* populations. Much is unknown. In principle, both the hereditarian and environmentalist interpretations are possible, but once one gets down to details these two labels are only a hindrance and have to be discarded (indeed one of the tricks used by participants in the debate has been to assume that everyone has to be either a hereditarian or an environmentalist and then to draw the dividing line between the two in the position which best suits his own case!). The serious student who is trying to clear up some of the problems we have described may well deny that he is either a hereditarian or an environmentalist. The scientific middle ground is so extensive that it is only mischievous to force the diversity of viewpoints in this debate into two over-simplified categories.

The evidence indicates that there are substantial IQ differences between people. It is important to recognise that even where the existence of genetic differences between individuals or groups is well established, manipulation of the environment can potentially have enormous effects on phenotypes. Firstly, as we saw in Fig 2, a change in some environmental factor can sometimes erase, or even reverse, a phenotypic difference even between two genetically distinct groups. The difference between the rat strains in maze-running ability, so apparent when the rats are reared in normal environments, should not be construed as an unalterable performance difference merely because it is based on genetic differences between the strains. For when both strains are reared in 'stimulating' environments, the former performance gap essentially disappears. Thus even if the black-white IQ gap were known to be partly genetic, we could not *a priori* exclude the possibility that environmental innovation in the US could have a comparable impact on the IQ gap.

Secondly, present heritability estimates for IQ only tell us how important individual genetic differences are, given the *existing* range of environments in contemporary North American and north-west European societies. They can tell us nothing about how important genetic differences for IQ will be in ten years' time if we have in the meantime devised new forms of environmental intervention. We can illustrate this point by considering resistance to an infectious disease like smallpox. One hundred years ago differences between individuals in respect of contracting smallpox probably had a substantial heritability; inherited resistance to the disease would be a relatively important explanation for who caught smallpox and who did not. Nowadays with methods of environmental intervention such as immunisation and/or public health controls heritability is undoubtedly lower; most of the differences between people in contracting this disease will depend on differences in exposure to (or immunisation against) smallpox.

Thirdly, much has been learned from the treatment of the so-called 'genetic diseases' like phenylketonuria, diabetes, and galactosemia. Rare genes contribute to all of these debilitating conditions yet by manipulating the patient's internal biochemical environment (as by injections or control of his diet), his phenotype can be made virtually normal. In this way novel environments have been designed which compensate for genetic disadvantages.

Thus genetic differences do not preclude environmental intervention, and the important task is to improve the conditions of life for children of all colours and backgrounds and to assist each one to make the most of his potential. How we should do that is often problematic. Some people believe that the English comprehensive school discriminates against the most gifted children by forcing them to go at the pace of their age mates instead of going at the pace that is natural to them. Whether girls should receive a different education is another controversial issue. The question of how to help children suffering from the disadvantages to which their parents and grandparents were subjected is not an easy one to answer, but it is a vitally important one to tackle.

It would not be surprising if genetically controlled IQ differences were discovered between populations in different regions of the world or originating from them. Equally, as our discussion of the place of plasticity in evolution should have suggested, it would not be surprising if no differences were found: there is no reason to believe that genetic differences in brain structure would necessarily express themselves in IQ scores. Human beings adapt by both organic and superorganic processes to their environment. A significant part of the environment to which our children must adapt is the IQ test itself. But these tests as we know them have been constructed to classify individuals in ways our present society finds useful. Had our social priorities been different, different kinds of test would have been constructed. As Jensen observes,

> If the content and instructional techniques of education had been markedly different from what they were in the beginning and, for the most part, continue to be, it is very likely that the instruments we call intelligence tests would also have assumed a quite different character. They might have developed in such a way as to measure a quite different constellation of abilities, and our conception of the nature of intelligence, assuming we still called it by that name, would be correspondingly different.

We have therefore to ask whether we want to educate children to live in our society as it is now, or to educate them for a better society. If we want a better society, maybe we want less acquisitiveness, less individualism, more gaiety and more good fellowship. In that event, we may need different tests. We come back to the basic question: what are IQ tests *for*?

Chapter 5

RACE AND BEHAVIOUR

We have now reviewed evidence about differences in the anatomy and physiology of geographical races and have considered the origins of racial differences in biology and culture. The suggestion that these racial differences include brain size or structural differences which cause variations in intelligence has also been examined. It is now necessary to consider whether differences in the evolutionary history of geographical races may have given rise to differences in behaviour of a more far-reaching kind than those assessed by intelligence tests. We have also to ask whether there are any genetically determined patterns of behaviour which are relevant to theories of race relations. The most obvious of these is the claim that humans, like other animals, show a 'natural' preference for their 'own kind' and a 'natural' antagonism towards other kinds which tend to preserve races as separate inbreeding populations.

For the biologist forms of behaviour constitute a particular class of trait. Like all anatomical or physiological traits, behaviours are influenced by the organism's genotype. Largely since World War II, research in a new field in biology—behaviour genetics—has demonstrated that behavioural predispositions are apparently inherited according to much the same basic rules as have been worked out for other animal and plant traits. The expression of these behavioural genotypes is also influenced by the environment. Each animal possesses a variety of behavioural options encoded in its genes; the various environmental stimuli to which the animal is exposed decide which of these options will be taken up.

GENES AND ANIMAL BEHAVIOUR

Genetic influences on animal behaviour are usually demonstrated in two ways. First, as we saw with the maze-running ability of rats (Chapter 4), we can breed animals which have been selected for a particular behavioural characteristic. If, after several generations of such selection, our resulting strain differs significantly (in the trait selected) from the animals we started with, we have evidence of a genetic basis for that trait. Second, we can choose two inbred animal strains that were originally bred for some non-behavioural trait (perhaps coat colour, resistance to disease, size etc) and rear them under identical conditions. Since the two strains differ genetically to a considerable extent as reflected in their anatomical and physiological differences, we can ask whether they also differ for a particular behavioural trait. If they do, we again have evidence of genes influencing that behavioural trait. (An even more dramatic demonstration of this can be made by testing two related *species* reared in the same environment.)

Many examples of such strain differences in behaviour could be cited including preference in mice for (or aversion towards) alcohol, emotionality and hoarding behaviour in rats and mice, the tendency in chickens and mice to dominate others of the same species, and aggressiveness in many species. In one well-known study five different breeds of puppy were born and reared under the same conditions and tested for various kinds of social behaviour during the first year of life. The breeds differed widely (though always with some overlap between them) not only in their behaviour at any given age but also in the pattern of their behavioural changes during growth and development. Among the traits for which breed differences were found are dominance (assessed by the willingness of the puppy to compete for, and defend, his food against others), the tendency for bitches to retrieve puppies removed from their litter, emotionality (tail-wagging, biting, barking), leash trainability, and ability to solve a variety of specific problems. Even on very general learning tasks differences between breeds soon became apparent in the particular ways each breed elected to adapt to a given situation. For example, in order that their weights could be accurately determined, young puppies had to be taught to remain still on the scale for a short while. As the puppies learned to meet this requirement, the experimenters noticed that an increasing percentage of cocker spaniels adapted by *sitting* peacefully on the scale while basenjis and fox terriers remained *standing* and struggled. The breeds even differed in 'learning style'; faced with a given task to be learned, shetland sheep dogs tended to form *habits* early on and stick to them throughout subsequent learning trials while beagles tended to *vary* continually the methods they used to perform the task. Despite considerable breed differences on individual tasks, however, the overall problem-solving performance of each breed was about the same.*

In some animal species, especially among insects, certain behaviours seem to be determined purely by inheritance. For example there is a species of wasp in which the female, when ready to lay an egg, goes in search of a host. She always chooses one particular species of the tarantula spider, digs a hole in front of it, and then attacks until her sting finds a chink in its armour. When the spider has been stunned, the wasp drags it into the hole, lays her egg in its abdomen and covers over the hole. She has never seen this done before, thus learning appears not to be involved. This is the kind of 'automatic' behaviour that is often called instinctive. Even in insects, however, learning occurs with some traits; bees and ants learn to recognise members of their own colony through their scent.

If we consider animals with larger and more 'human-like' brains, we find that in general the development of their behaviours is influenced increasingly by learning. Still further along this spectrum, learning accounts for so many individual *human* differences that it becomes far more difficult to find instinctive behaviours.

* Evidence of this kind is one of the reasons why so many behaviour geneticists have for years been trying to replace the use of 'general intelligence' tests by a battery of tests, each of which measures only a very specific mental ability.

But in what ways do heredity and environment influence behaviour? Basically heredity seems to place constraints on the *time* during development when the animal is responsive to certain environmental stimuli as well as on the *extent* to which a given behaviour can be shaped by those stimuli. If we consider first the acquisition of songs by young birds, we see that the rigidity of inherited constraints on this trait varies widely among species. Song sparrows, isolated from other song sparrows and foster-reared by canaries, still acquire their characteristic song. (The song sparrow is 'pre-programmed' with his song.) Somewhat less rigidly programmed, the fledgling white-crowned sparrow needs to hear the adult model of its song during a *sensitive period* in its development in order to acquire its song; if the fledgling is exposed during this period not only to adult members of its own species but also to birds of other neighbouring species, it still learns only its own song. (Thus the fledgling white-crowned sparrow inherits a predisposition to respond but only to 'appropriate' stimuli.) Even less rigidly programmed, meadowlarks, when isolated from their own kind as fledglings, acquire the song of the species by whom they are fostered. (Thus the fledgling meadowlark also inherits a predisposition to respond but to a wider range of stimuli.) Lastly the goldfinch even as an adult can learn new songs from other species. (The goldfinch's predisposition to respond to a wide range of stimuli is not restricted to the fledgling stage of its development.)

'Imprinting', a phenomenon first identified among fowl species, also illustrates the kinds of limits which heredity and environment place on behavioural development. While studying the greylag goose some forty years ago, Konrad Lorenz discovered that the goslings would follow around the first moving thing they saw after hatching, even if it was Lorenz himself! Despite their subsequent interaction with other geese, they remained strongly attached to their 'substitute mother' into adulthood and sometimes preferred to court the imprinted object rather than other geese. Typically the newly hatched bird can only be imprinted in this way during a narrowly defined stage of development: in the chick this sensitive period occurs about thirteen to fourteen hours after hatching, and imprinting is practically impossible by thirty hours. Sensitive periods for social behaviour have also been studied in mammals. For example at about three weeks of age puppies become extremely attached to the creatures with which they interact. If a puppy is removed from its litter early in this period and reared by man, its major adult relationships will be with humans, and it will pay little attention to other dogs. The longer one waits before removing the puppy from its litter, the stronger will be its eventual relationships with dogs and the weaker its relationships with humans. Genes determine the timing of sensitive periods because even different strains of the same species often have different sensitive periods for the same trait.

The rearing environment may also influence an animal's predatory behaviour. Many people would consider that it is instinctive for a cat to chase and kill rats. Yet a series of classic experiments showed that while kittens kill the kinds of rat which they see their mothers kill, kittens raised in isolation do not necessarily learn to kill rats. Some kittens were raised in the same cages with rats and they never killed their cage-mates. The kittens would let the rats run about in the cage, climb over their backs or heads, eat from the same dish and often allow the rats to pull meat or fish from their mouths. Similar results were obtained when kittens were raised in cages with adult sparrows. In addition studies have shown that the opportunity for young birds to play with nest-building material and young monkeys to play with each other was essential if they were to develop into normal adults.

GENES AND HUMAN BEHAVIOUR

Because man shares much of his physiology and some, at least, of his genes with other animals, it is reasonable to assume that some human behaviours will also be under genetic control. As we saw in Chapter 4, this assumption is borne out in the case of IQ.

In respect of intellectual abilities generally, it is known that several forms of mental retardation are caused by single gene defects, among them phenylketonuria. Chromosome abnormalities can also affect mental ability, as in the case of the children who used to be called 'mongoloid' but are now said to suffer from 'Down's syndrome'. Some personality traits also appear to be substantially influenced by genes. Identical twins reared in different families are still more similar along the dimensions of 'extroversion-introversion' and neuroticism than are fraternal twins reared in the same family. Tests also show identical twins to be more alike than fraternal twins on measures of 'need for achievement' and shyness. Even with babies under one year of age, twin studies have indicated that smiling and fear of a stranger are genetically influenced.

A great deal of data has been gathered on the contributions of heredity and environment to the development of mental illness, the great bulk of it concerned with schizophrenia. There is no doubt that environmental factors contribute to schizophrenia; this can be seen from the discovery that even among identical twins rarely more than 70 per cent of the twin pairs will be 'concordant' (ie either *both* schizophrenic or *both* 'normal'). Nevertheless the concordance rate for identical twins—no matter how low—is almost always significantly greater than the rate for fraternal twins, thus implicating genetic factors. One study supporting this conclusion matched (a) a group of children (born of schizophrenic mothers) who were given up for adoption at birth with (b) a comparison group of children (born of non-psychotic mothers) who were given up for adoption at about the same time. Several decades later these children were tracked down by the investigator who found that significantly more of the 'a group' than of the 'b group' had become schizophrenic.

Several studies indicate that identical twins are substantially more concordant than fraternal twins on certain indices of criminality. Similar data also suggest the involvement of genetic as well as environmental factors in some forms of homosexuality.

Although the evidence is far from complete, by and large behaviour geneticists regard all human behaviours as *influenced* in some way by genes though not completely *determined* by genes.

All behaviours are seen as the outcome of a variety of human genotypes interacting with a variety of physical and social stimuli in the environment. The next problem is to find out *how* genes are able to exert their effects on behaviour. Let us examine two systems in the body that are of prime importance in behaviour: the nervous system (especially the brain) and the endocrine system of glands and the hormones they produce. Recall that each constituent of the cells in each system in the body has its composition encoded in the genes. Variations in these constituents will affect the overall properties of the system. Behaviours associated with brain functioning—such as mental abilities and personality characteristics—will thus be influenced by inherited variations in brain structure.

Hormones—messenger molecules which regulate chemical activities in the body—are particularly relevant to emotional behaviours. Experiments with guinea pigs and monkeys have demonstrated that when a male sex hormone is given to pregnant female animals, the female offspring of these mothers (compared to the female offspring of untreated mothers) are more likely to display characteristically 'male behaviour': to threaten, initiate action and engage in rough play. It has also been found that castration of male rats (thus lowering their blood levels of male sex hormones) led, following the age of puberty, to the display of 'female behaviour': the castrated males allowed intact males to mount them. Comparable evidence exists for man. A number of findings suggest that the depression, mood swings, tension and irritability that many women experience immediately prior to and during menstruation as well as in the first week or two after having given birth, may be caused by the large decreases at these times in the level of the hormone progesterone in the blood stream. It seems clear that hormone variations affect behaviour in both animals and man.

As we mentioned in Chapter 2, the release of hormones into the blood stream can be triggered by environmental stimuli. In mice, for example, the reproductive cycle (which is regulated by sex hormones) can be accelerated by exposing females to the smell of male mice. In several wild animal species seasonal changes in mating behaviour are thought to be due to changes in sex hormone levels which, in turn, are triggered off by the seasonal changes in the length of daylight. In monkeys the blood level of the largely male sex hormone, testosterone, correlates both with the amount of aggressive behaviour the animal displays in a monkey group and with the animal's rank in the group's pecking order; in the light of this, it is interesting that lowered levels of testosterone were found in male monkeys when they were removed from a group where they were among the socially dominant 'élite' to one where their claims to dominance were rejected. Similarly, lowered testosterone levels were found among male officer candidates in the United States Navy at an early stage of their training when they were subjected to considerable harassment by their seniors. It may be, then, that in man and other primates levels of this hormone are depressed by the individual's experience of humiliation or domination. Lastly, in laboratory experiments where subjects were shown full-length films which made them angry, agitated or anxious, the subjects produced more of the hormone adrenalin during the films than before or afterwards. Their response to relatively unemotive documentary films of natural scenery, on the other hand, was to produce less adrenalin than before or afterwards. In general, humans react to stress—whether physical or psychological—by producing more adrenalin and other hormones of the adrenal gland.

While environmental stimuli thus influence behaviour via hormones, genes also influence behaviour, again by virtue of the fact that all the components of a hormone system are made according to genetic instructions. The structure of the hormone molecule itself is genetically coded; tiny differences in the genes for 'hormone X' in two individuals (or breeds of animal) could alter the characteristics of their hormone X molecules, leading to consequent behavioural differences between the individuals or breeds concerned (all other things being equal). In similar fashion, genes probably affect the rate of construction of a hormone, its release from its gland into the blood stream, and the responsiveness of its target cells to it. Inherited variations in all these gene-coded processes are thought to have potential behavioural consequences.

One model of this kind which is currently guiding research on humans can be illustrated with reference to the thyroid gland. Release of the thyroid hormone, thyroxin, is known to increase following psychological stress. This is probably an important mechanism in helping the body to cope with stress because persons who have had their thyroid gland removed often develop mental illness (and their symptoms can sometimes be relieved by giving them thyroxin). This, along with the finding of common personality patterns in patients who over-produce thyroxin, suggest that thyroxin release can have behavioural consequences. A variety of thyroid deficiencies resulting in the under-production of thyroxin are known to be hereditary. Individual differences within the *normal* range for thyroxin level are also probably partially genetic in origin (for one or more of the reasons given in the previous paragraph). Under ordinary living conditions an individual who produces thyroxin at the lower end of the normal range is unlikely to experience any difficulties. When faced with prolonged psychological stress (and the attendant need to produce high levels of thyroxin), however, this individual—unlike others in the normal range—may become disadvantaged because of his thyroid genotype and as a consequence develop some form of mental illness. Here then is a model which illustrates how genetic factors can predispose an individual to certain behaviours which are only expressed in response to particular environmental stimuli. It shows how genes could account for individual differences in behavioural response to a given situation.

Quite often genetic and environmental explanations of a trait seem to be sharply at odds. The geneticist points out how a certain kind of mental illness for example is hereditary; the environmentalist points out how that illness is brought on by psychological stress. It is sometimes overlooked that (1) even with identical twins reared together in the same family concordance for mental illness is usually well below 100 per cent and (2) not all persons exposed to severe psychological stress develop mental illness. These two types of apparently *competing* explanation can, however, be quite readily shown to *complement* one another by using the kind of model we have just described above.

GENES AND POPULATION DIFFERENCES IN BEHAVIOUR

As anthropologists have been showing for decades, a great number, perhaps most, of the behavioural differences between populations are 'cultural' in origin; such behaviours are transferred from older to younger generations through the process of learning. It is common knowledge that when persons are removed from one cultural setting to another—as happened, for example, on a large scale in the United States in the early twentieth century—they tend to adapt and acquire behaviours characteristic of their new environment. Unlike insect species, they tend not to retain stubbornly the behaviour patterns appropriate only to their former milieu.

We have explained, however, that every population—whether defined in terms of physical features, cultural practices or social characteristics etc—is almost certain to differ from every other population in the frequency of one or more of its genes. And genes, as should by now be clear, affect many types of human behaviour. Therefore, we now want to consider whether any of the behavioural differences between human populations (and in particular between geographical races) may be affected by gene frequency differences between those populations.*

Connections of this kind are quite plausible from a genetic point of view but are still highly speculative. In this section we want to carry this speculation as far as we reasonably can and then ask 'which behavioural differences between populations could this possibly explain?' As we noted in Chapter 3, social

* Some readers may feel that such enquiry is dangerous since it can be used to give apparent respectability to the very doctrines we have been criticising. They should note that modern biological research is subjected to very much tighter professional control than was possible a century ago. The political exploitation of biological findings is now much more difficult and biologists are more alert to such dangers.

and cultural practices can affect gene frequencies in a population via their influence on breeding patterns within (or outside) the population. During the evolution of *Homo sapiens*, man's newly acquired cultural practices are thought to have hastened his organic evolution by giving individuals with appropriate traits a selective advantage. This means that if two human populations, derived from the same stock, have maintained different cultural practices for perhaps a few thousand years or more, it is quite conceivable that these populations now differ significantly in their frequencies for genes relevant to the cultural practices concerned. If both populations were now to be transplanted into a new environment foreign to both of them, they would presumably adapt to the new environment using those cultural practices to which most members' genes predisposed them. Analogous to this phenomenon are the different behavioural strategies used by fox terriers and cocker spaniels to adapt to the requirement that they 'stay put' on the scale during weighing.

Consider the following case in man. Human milk contains a kind of sugar (lactose) which the vast majority of infant mammals can (indeed, *must*, if they rely on breast feeding) digest. Beyond infancy most (85–95 per cent) Europeans continue to be capable of digesting lactose, but most (85–100 per cent) individuals in American Indian, African, Asian and Australian Aboriginal populations do *not*. As it turns out, children and adults in the latter populations by and large lack the gene for lactose digestion. When persons lacking this gene drink milk, the lactose passes right through them undigested, and they may suffer moderate discomfort. How are these population differences in gene frequency to be explained? The exceptions to the generalisations made above offer a clue. African and Asian populations which keep herds of milk-producing animals *can* digest lactose, and southern European populations are *less* likely than other European ones to be able to digest lactose. Apparently, therefore, populations with (or with a history of) this type of pastoral economy have genotypes which foster milk consumption while populations lacking this pastoral tradition also lack the genetic equipment for milk consumption. It is thought that about 10,000–12,000 years ago, as some human populations began to domesticate milk-producing animals, a selective advantage accrued to those individuals in such populations who could use this milk as a food. In this way the genes and cultural practices of a population would have been brought into alignment. Interestingly, at least one study has indicated that in the United States black school children were significantly less likely than white school children to finish their lunchtime milk. Here, then, is an example where population differences in culture or behaviour may reflect parallel underlying genetic predispositions.

Geographic races are known to differ in the frequency of at least four other genes which influence behaviour. Like lactose digestion, however, each of these traits is determined by only one or two genes; thus genes affecting the more genetically complex and socially important behavioural traits (eg intelligence, personality etc) have not yet been shown to differ in frequency in various geographical races. The four traits are albinism, colour-blindness, the ability to taste PTC (a chemical) and phenylketonuria. Albinism affects behaviour in that those who suffer from it avoid bright light. Colour-blindness and PTC-tasting ability have comparable, if minor, consequences for similar reasons. Only phenylketonuria is of obvious social significance, and even here the proportion of each population affected is very small: in England 0·4 per cent of the population are affected, in Ireland 1·4 per cent and in non-European populations this defect is generally very rare (eg in Japan only 0·02 per cent are affected).

All the known differences between geographical races in the frequency of genes which affect behaviour are therefore quite trivial. Yet in principle it is possible that there may be genetic differences affecting socially, politically or economically significant behaviours and it seems reasonable to expect that the more population geneticists and physical anthropologists look for such genetic differences, the more will they discover. Because, however, of (1) the relative plasticity of human behaviour, (2) the genetic heterogeneity of all human populations, and

(3) the mass of data suggesting the importance of situational determinants (eg economic and political factors) in explaining race relations, there is at present little reason to expect that a substantial part of intergroup relations will ever be explicable in genetic terms.

The discussion in this chapter so far has been restricted primarily to *known* gene frequency differences between geographical races. In this respect we have been approaching the question of racial differences in behaviour from 'underneath' (or from a 'reductionist' perspective). But we can also approach the question from 'above', looking down on to races from a broad evolutionary perspective. Using this approach one might argue as follows: (1) Different evolutionary pressures have produced extensive animal *species* differences in behaviour, some of which serve as general mechanisms for the species' survival; (2) geographical races of man have also been subject to different evolutionary pressures; (3) man is also an animal; therefore perhaps one can extrapolate from species to races and from other animals to man in order to argue the plausibility both of extensive racial differences in behaviour and of biological mechanisms for racial survival. This approach is obviously much more speculative and capable of misuse than the approach from underneath. It also has a long history, and for these reasons we want now to examine it.

THE EVOLUTION OF ANIMAL BEHAVIOUR

Social Darwinist writing placed great stress on organic evolution as a means of explaining social patterns. This line of thought tended from the outset to emphasise the ways in which competition within or between species could facilitate natural selection, and to neglect the part played by co-operative activity and by superorganic evolution. The one-sidedness of these arguments arose partly from the writers' enthusiasm for a new theory and partly from an error. Darwin, like others of his generation, believed that the biological inheritance of a child involved the blending of elements from the parents. The child's characters would be about half way between the parents'. This meant that any genetic variation appearing in one generation would be drastically reduced in the next, so that if natural selection was to favour adaptive variations it had to act fast. Mendel's law of particulate inheritance revised this theory; it showed that selection could achieve its results at a gentler pace and that there was less need to seek to preserve adaptive variation by eugenic measures than the theory of blending inheritance implied. Reacting to the incautious manner in which Darwin's theories were extended, some subsequent writers have unduly minimised the physical nature of man in their desire to stress instead the extent to which by conscious decision he can create more equal and harmonious societies.

A series of recent books has popularised the fascinating research that has been conducted into patterns of social behaviour amongst animals. Among them should be mentioned Konrad Lorenz's *On Aggression*, Robert Ardrey's *The Territorial Imperative* and Desmond Morris's *The Naked Ape*. Their arguments differ, but their general tendency (especially with the two authors first named) is to contend that the pendulum has swung too far and that the importance of organic evolution is now being under-valued. Much of what they say, or imply, about the behaviour of man, consists of conjectures based on the results of animal studies, but this does not mean that it should not be seriously considered. Conjecture plays an essential part in science, telling a research worker where to look in order to find theoretically significant evidence. Nor should popular works or studies by informed amateurs be disparaged, for the task of explaining knowledge in simple terms sometimes helps lay bare its assumptions; the amateur may bring out an aspect that is obscured by the specialist's blinkers.

In assessing what such studies have to teach us, it is well to remember our description, in Chapter 1, of natural selection as a process by which those members of a population which are best adapted to their environment contribute more to future generations than those which are less well endowed. We pointed out subsequently that adaptation can be achieved by specialisation or by developing plasticity. The ultimate result of adaptation and selection can be the appearance of a species, which is a group of actually or potentially interbreeding natural populations. It is still uncertain quite how many species have been produced in this way for there are many that remain to be described by biologists, but it seems probable that there are over 850,000 insect species, and over 1 million animal species altogether. The significance of plasticity in the evolution of man may be seen from comparison with birds. Man is one species. Birds form a cluster of 8,500 species. Birds have evolved by specialisation, developing a variety of species each adapted to a particular ecological 'niche'. Robins, blackbirds, thrushes and other birds can forage without friction in overlapping territories; in many cases they seek different kinds of food. Man has evolved by developing a capacity for culture which enables him to inhabit virtually every one of the earth's terrestrial niches; he has not divided into distinct sub-categories unable to interbreed.

There are basic differences in the way man has adapted his behavioural patterns to his habitat by comparison with other animal species. Behaviour patterns which in non-human animals are instinctive or involve very little learning may in man be largely learned. Man's capacity for learning has a genetic base (in the design of the nervous system) but the particular behaviours which any individual man acquires are only very loosely constrained by genetic factors. For example, man's capacity for language is genetically controlled, but as far as we know a man who can learn one language can also learn another (though there are a few which present special difficulties of pronunciation). This is not the case, as we saw earlier, with the learning of calls among some bird species. Because man has this capacity for learning his behavioural adaptations to particular environments can be changed relatively quickly.

These differences in the evolutionary status of species are of particular importance if conclusions are drawn from animal studies for application to man. The popular ethologists have not always been sufficiently careful in this connection. Evidence about the cat is of more value, other things being equal, than evidence about the rat, for the cat has a larger brain and learning capacity. A form of behaviour which is genetically determined in the rat will not necessarily be genetically determined in the cat. There is a better chance that what is genetic in the cat will be so in the rat also, but even this can only be assumed. In addition different strains of the *same species* do not always share the same gene-based behaviour patterns. Evidence about insects is of least value because their behavioural patterns are so often instinctive. Evidence about non-human primates—especially apes and monkeys—is of the greatest value because his fellow primates are closest to man's evolution and man shares more of his genetic inheritance with them than with other kinds of species.

There has been a lively controversy in recent years about the extent to which aggression among humans is to be understood as the outcome of the same factors as those which appear to explain its incidence among non-human animals. Some writers argue that it is usually by establishing control over a territory and its food resources that evolutionary success becomes possible. This is because the animals who control a territory are more likely to mate successfully. Behavioural characteristics (like aggression) which help an animal to acquire and maintain a territory, will allow him to contribute more of his genes to future generations. Such reasoning explains the title of Konrad Lorenz's book in the original German, *Das Sogenannte Böse*, the so-called evil. He maintains that aggression between animals of the *same* species (ie intra-specific) is not really evil but good because in the first place it causes all members of the species to spread themselves out and make maximum use of the area available to them. In the second place, aggressive behaviour means that the strongest males get priority with the females, siring more offspring than other males. In the third place it provides animal communities with the most effective champions to protect the herd (and particularly its young) against attack. Yet, according to Lorenz, these are only the more obvious benefits that aggressiveness brings to a species. It is also a basic drive, a release of stored energy, which lies behind behaviour patterns, including personal friendship and love, those that outwardly have nothing to do with aggression. A personal bond is found only in animals with highly developed intra-specific aggression; the firmer the bond, the more aggressive is the species, and both may vary according to the season. This suggests that the personal bond may have developed at that phase of evolution when, in aggressive animals, the co-operation of male and female was needed for the tending of the brood.

Lorenz has surprisingly little to say about aggression between animals of *different* species (ie inter-specific), indeed it falls outside his definition of aggression as 'the fighting instinct in beast and man which is directed against members of the same species'. When a predator falls upon his prey, this is not aggression but simply a way of feeding. When the potential prey seeks to fight back, in the way birds may mob an owl, a cat or a fox, this is closer to aggression but still a different phenomenon. There are also circumstances in which an animal, like a cornered rat, will attack anything that appears to threaten it. In all these cases the attacking animal has an obvious advantage to gain and it is not—or so it would seem from Lorenz's account—necessary to explain them in the same terms as intra-specific aggression.

Konrad Lorenz has been one of the great pioneers of the study of animal behaviour and his remarkable achievements have deservedly brought him a Nobel Prize. Yet his fellow specialists advance trenchant criticisms when discussing the selective way in which he draws upon the available evidence. Professor R. A. Hinde of Cambridge refers to his 'ignoring the bulk of the experimental literature on his subject'. The behaviour geneticist John Paul Scott expresses a similar reservation, 'he is a very narrow specialist, who primarily knows the behaviour of birds . . . he evidently reads very little other than material which is directly related to his own speciality.' Other writers complain about his reference to 'the bloody mass battles of the brown rat', observing that nothing of the sort appears in the detailed accounts of this species, and to his apparently quite unjustifiable statements about the alleged violent behaviour of the Ute Indians of Colorado. One of the great lessons that have been learned in animal behaviour studies during the past twenty years is that it is not legitimate to generalise about behaviour from studies of animals held captive in zoos. The restricted space available to caged animals, and their inability to develop the families and groupings that characterise them in the wild, have a profound effect upon their behaviour. They mutilate themselves, masturbate, attack their offspring, develop stomach ulcers, become fetishists, suffer from obesity, form homosexual pair-bonds and commit murder (to quote Desmond Morris's gory list). In some species they will not breed. Lorenz knows this as well as anyone, but he can forget it. As one ethologist remarks, 'he has done most of his research with tamed animals, such as geese induced by guard fences and food to live in a human environment, and with captive cichlid fishes in tanks. All creatures so confined have their aggressiveness heightened enormously.'

Robert Ardrey's book draws heavily on Lorenz's approach. It seeks to establish, firstly, that there are certain territorial species in which the behaviour of all males, and sometimes of females too, is governed by an inherent drive to gain and defend an area of space, whether of water, earth or air. In most but not all territorial species, defence is directed only against fellow members of the species. We will consider this claim before turning to his second one, which is that man 'is as much a territorial animal as is a mocking bird singing in the clear California night'.

Ardrey makes it clear that some species, like elephants, gorillas and grazing animals generally, are not territorial. Other species, through long evolutionary trial and error, have come to incorporate into their behaviour a disposition to possess a territory which often becomes effective at the time they attain sexual maturity. He recognises difficulties in defining an instinct, a drive or a disposition, but insists that, whatever it be called, the phenomenon he describes is real and important. When he speaks of aggression he means simply a disposition to dominate, preferring to consider separately aggression that utilises violence. Like Lorenz, Ardrey draws attention to the way animals recognise the rights of territorial ownership and withdraw when threatened by the owner. This is important to his argument about aggression in man for he remarks that 'the problem of man is not that we are aggressive but that we break the rules'. Animals have ways of signalling defeat that prevent the aggression of the dominant one being translated into actual violence. Ardrey writes in an easy, non-technical manner presenting examples which will carry conviction with the ordinary reader. But ethology is now a specialised field of research and we need to turn to experts to hear whether the situation is as simple as it appears to be and whether the writer is carefully distracting attention from examples and other evidence which conflicts with his argument.

Ardrey's synthesis of the evidence about territoriality has been reviewed by John Hurrell Crook who concludes—as specialists are so apt to do—with words like 'Yes, but . . .' Crook does not object to the proposition that there are territorial species but explains that things are not quite so simple. There is much diversity between species and within species, so that the active defence of true territories represents only one extreme of the continuum of territoriality. Territorial behaviour can arise only when there are two or more animals, so it is misleading to think of it in terms of the individual's motives without considering the way groups of individuals come to work out a pattern of territories. In many species, individuals maintain regular spaces around themselves from which they try to expel intruders; repeated encounters give rise to pecking orders. It is not easy to disentangle the maintenance of personal space from the possession of territory, and Crook believes that when the various contributory factors have been separated it will no longer be helpful to discuss this behaviour as if it were the product of a single drive or instinct. There are already many advantages in seeing it as a feature of the social system of a particular species which varies as the system varies, for example with the different seasons of the year. Again, there is evidence from many species (and particularly from monkeys) that differences in upbringing can significantly affect aggressiveness. Other authors, notably Claire and W. M. S. Russell, maintain that violence and territoriality are to be seen not as the outcome of an invariant drive but as part of a complex of resources evolved to achieve drastic reduction of a population that is in danger of out-growing its resources. A male who cannot obtain a territory often cannot mate, and population growth is thereby limited.

EXTRAPOLATION TO MAN

The conclusions which scientists have drawn from the study of other species may well apply to humans also, but no one can be sure of this. It is essential to regard these propositions as hypotheses which must be tested on humans before they are supposed relevant to human problems. Testing is not easily done, even in the study of infants, or psychologically retarded children, because *Homo sapiens* is so complicated a species and there are moral limitations upon the kind of research that is acceptable. It is equally essential to formulate these propositions precisely. To say that territory is important in human affairs is not to claim anything new. To assert that man is a territorial animal is a mischievous extravagance when those who advance it fail to specify just what such a classification implies and what they consider the critical evidence for classifying a species as territorial or not. It is mischievous because other people outside the scientific community are likely to use the statement for purposes that may be distinct from the scientists'. We know what damage was done when racial classifications were abused for political ends. It would be inexcusable were the mistake to be repeated with the preliminary findings of animal studies.

There is concern that the writings of Lorenz and Ardrey are already being interpreted in terms of a political philosophy which assumes that man is inherently depraved and that therefore authoritarian government is necessary. Before these books had been published, at a 1963 symposium of the Institute of Biology in London, two distinguished zoologists positively stated that 'man is a territorial animal'. One of them seemed to think he had substantiated his judgement by saying 'you have only to notice the signboards dotted all over the countryside announcing that "Trespassers will be prosecuted" to realise this'. His inference was as worthless as the signboards (in England there are no prosecutions for trespass as it is a civil offence; in Scotland there is no such offence). Very few Englishmen possess any territory on which to erect such boards; are *they* territorial? If they suddenly become rich how many of them buy land and have their boundaries marked in this way? Most men display a concern for an area of personal space and a sensitivity about personal property, but among humans territory appears to be simply one form of property, and probably not the most important. Human society includes rules designed to limit incursions upon personal space and upon ownership, but these are only one set of rules among many other kinds of rules.

Biologists approach questions like this from two very different perspectives. On the one hand they conduct detailed observations of the species in question. On the other, they develop conjectural explanations of the form and behaviour of species in terms of the way it has evolved, or use evolutionary conjectures to formulate hypotheses for testing. Because of the difficulty of observing human behaviour systematically, the conjectures sometimes are given undue prominence. In the field of race there is one hypothesis towards which biologists seem to be attracted as moths to a candle. It concerns the evolutionary value of prejudice, intra-specific aggression, or antagonism towards those who do not belong to the individual's group. They observe that in the early stages of his evolution man may have been very dependent on co-operative activity to compete with other mammals for food and to defend himself from predators. There may also have been competition between human groups. In such circumstances there would have been a strong selective pressure favouring individuals who identified with their fellows and who were psychologically prepared for struggles with outsiders. These writers then suggest that contemporary race prejudice may be at least in part an expression of the same mechanism; an instinct left over from an earlier situation in which it had survival value; an evolutionary hangover which expresses itself more strongly when members of other groups are of different outward appearance.

This conjecture was set forth in eloquent prose in a lecture by Sir Arthur Keith which carried forward Gumplowicz's conception of race-building and of group sentiment as a prime influence upon mating patterns. In recent years it has been rehearsed by C. D. Darlington. Before considering specific criticisms it is well to locate it within a rather special class of statements. For the difficulty with generalising about evolution is that it is a process that has happened just once. With relatively few exceptions it is impossible to compare evolutionary change with anything else, or to say what would have happened had one of the components been absent. Therefore everything has its place in evolution: prejudice, pain, crime and so on. If everything has its place then, by implication, everything is justified.

Because we know so little about the distant past it has not been easy to submit these speculations to the discipline of fact. However there are some ways of checking up on Keith's theory. Animal behaviour studies cast doubt on the assumption that early man lived in closed groups. When two gorilla groups meet in the forest they do not behave aggressively and individuals appear to be free to join or leave a group at will. Among chimpanzees, group membership is always fluctuating and groups or individuals can roam freely through the forest. This capacity of apes (as opposed to monkeys) to live in open groups, with a membership varying according to circumstance and individual inclination, may be a clue to the adaptation that was required of man's ancestors when they left the forest and took to hunting in open country. Certainly the hunting and gathering societies in the contemporary world (which one may take as a prototype of early human society) do not have rigid rules about band membership; they respond in a friendly way to contacts with other groups and abjure violence in the settlement of internal disputes. What evidence we have on this point therefore does not support a basic component in the theory.

Even if there were a genetically based disposition of the kind envisaged, it would still be necessary to show that it was activated by groups differentiated by race rather than in other ways. (Acute though the hostilities may sometimes be between the supporters of rival football teams, there is little ground to think that this influences mating patterns!) John Paul Scott has remarked that when strange dogs are introduced into a naturally formed group, most of the consequent antagonism is directed towards those of same sex and *similar breed*, and the least antagonism is directed towards members of the opposite sex and *different* breed. 'At the very least', he writes, 'there is no justification for the common belief that antagonism between unlike human beings is a "natural" phenomenon shared by other animals.'

W. M. S. Russell has observed that there are many examples of aggressive interaction within societies that are not divided into racial categories. The difficulty, he thinks, is that in the study of supposedly racial clashes we have no means of separating the factors of genetic divergence from those of cultural divergence, so that it is impossible to tell whether a genetic factor is a cause of the clash. He cites the case of the Greeks of classical times who were very uniform in physical appearance but split into societies with contrasting cultures. Warfare between them was endemic for several centuries. Another example is provided by the region of the Great Wall of China which was built along the dividing line between a society specialised increasingly in irrigation agriculture and, to the north, one devoted to pastoral nomadism. The Chinese sought to restrict trade across the frontier, built the wall, and had to contend with warfare that was almost continuous for 2,000 years although the peoples on either side of the line differed primarily in their cultural attributes. Russell therefore concludes that the most rewarding comparison is between the mutual hostility of animal populations between which the flow of genes is no longer possible and the hostility of human populations so divergent culturally that communication between them becomes difficult and restricted. When we understand enough about human cultural change it should therefore be possible to restore communication and peaceful interplay by economic, social and educational means. This is a suggestive formulation, because in the big cities of America and Europe intergroup hostility is most evident between groups that share a great deal culturally (rooted in industrial methods of production and the attendant styles of consumption) while diverging most in ways that make communication difficult. Political and economic differences can restrict communication substantially.

Indeed, if the student starts by plotting the patterns of contemporary racial tension he is unlikely to find that hostility is the greater the more the groups differ genetically. Whether the conflict in Northern Ireland is to be classified as a race relations situation is open to debate, but there is little argument that, religious and political issues apart, the opposing parties show strong resemblances. In the localities where racial tension is highest we find privileged groups seeking to justify and defend their advantages; we find unprivileged groups resentful of what seem to them unfair distinctions. When social systems pit one outwardly distinguishable group against another and give the two opposing interests any observer will expect hostility. It seems so obvious an explanation that many will think it unnecessary to look much further. Moreover, it is within most people's experience that the same individuals express prejudice of varying intensity according to circumstance, and that some individuals are much more prejudiced than others. Other factors are at work which cast doubt on any suggestion of a disposition supposedly innate in the species. The display of group aggression seems to conform to social patterns rather than to the release of pent-up aggression. In war-time most soldiers have to be motivated to attack the enemy (Frederick the Great, an enthusiastic militarist, insisted that a soldier must be taught to fear his officer more than an enemy). Television screens teach violence every day of the week, and political leaders regularly sanction it whenever it suits them. Studies in the United States have shown that ordinary citizens taking part in what appear to be scientific experiments are willing to inflict serious pain on their fellows so long as the experimenter assures them that it is part of the experiment. Competitive football games are not occasions for the release of accumulated energy so much as ceremonies in which spectators stimulate one another to more violent expression. The list is a long one. We have brought together rather different forms of behaviour to prevent it becoming too long, but long enough, we trust, to indicate the sorts of reason why students of intergroup conflict feel they have more potentially fruitful and immediate problems to examine than evolutionary conjectures.

One of the reasons for the divergence between the usual view sociologists take of prejudice and the biological hypothesis that it may serve an evolutionary function, is the time scale with which biologists are concerned. It took about 750,000 years for the species *Homo sapiens* to evolve out of *Homo erectus*. Since then evolutionary processes have been acting on populations of *Homo sapiens* for about 100,000 years without apparently producing any new human species. Sir Julian Huxley has concluded that evolution in man is not linear but reticulate or net-like; branches which have moved apart may come together again. In non-human species two sub-species which are brought together may either interbreed or clash; if they clash, it is aggression which changes them from being related sub-species to being separate species. In man there is reason to believe that inbreeding in separate geographical races is producing differences of the kind that characterise sub-species in non-human animals, but when geographical races are brought together there is usually considerable interbreeding. In that population of the United States which is conventionally accounted 'black', about 30 per cent of the gene pool is derived from white populations. In parts of Latin America previously distinctive races are disappearing year by year. With improved means of transport people who would previously have married spouses from their own locality are now mating with people from far away. On such grounds one may conclude that many racial divisions are melting away; if hostilities do occur along social lines marked by colour there are plenty of social factors which may explain them and the suggestion that members of the opposing groups are forbidden mates may actually encourage interbreeding.

As the key factor in the evolution of populations is relative success in producing offspring, a race prejudice that prevents the mixing of genes across group boundaries could increase genetic divergence between those groups. But there is no good evidence to substantiate claims that this kind of prejudice is innate. On the contrary it would seem that the relation of racial appearance to mating preferences is highly variable and greatly influenced by political conditions. It is not inevitable that it should become a factor causing different sections of humanity to move further apart genetically. There is nothing in evolution to make man follow the birds and divide into separate species.

Chapter 6

RACE AND DEMOCRACY

In the previous chapters we have discussed some of the respects in which human beings differ from one another. Some people are shorter than others, can lift less heavy weights, have poorer vision and below average IQ. It is easier to present our argument if we make a distinction between natural differences like these, and social inequalities which stem from the way societies are organised. This distinction has to be used with care, for the height, strength, vision and measured intelligence of children may be influenced by the diet of their mothers before birth, while the knowledge of what constitutes a good diet and the ability to pay for it are influenced by social factors. In some societies certain natural differences may be thought to justify social inequalities. The most obvious of these are associated with age. It is often assumed, without demonstration, that young people are less experienced and responsible than their seniors, and that old people deserve extra consideration because they have made their contributions to society. There are social processes which place a significance on natural differences so that people believe it 'natural' to defer to the elderly. It is not natural, and while a great majority might approve the custom of showing respect to seniors, there are many inequalities which are not justified by natural differences in the way people assume. In this chapter we will consider what account the government of a democratic society should take of natural differences in the population, but because so much of what appears to be natural is actually of social origin we shall have to discuss inequalities as well as differences.

The word 'democracy' refers to a set of arrangements whereby the government of a country is kept accountable to those who are governed. The key criterion is accountability. In one of the most famous statements of democratic belief, a funeral oration to the citizens of ancient Athens, Pericles declared, 'although only a few may originate a policy we are all able to judge it'. Judgement, and holding a government responsible, requires education. When the English government decided in the nineteenth century to give the vote to a wider range of citizens it recognised that it would have to provide for their education, for otherwise they would be unable to do their part. It may very well be that in most of the countries which today call themselves democracies citizens appear to cast their votes primarily in terms of self-interest, preferring the party which they think will do most to help themselves. This is not to say that they are completely unconcerned about the national interest or the long-term relations between different interest groups. Frequently they are required only to choose between a small number of political parties which differ in their appeal to various classes of voters but which share a similar commitment to the maintenance of the principles underlying the existing social order. Those countries come nearest to the democratic ideal in which the government is held accountable to the entire electorate because the voters believe that it should be concerned with the interests of the whole society.

The electorate is not the same as the population. In theory a democratic government is not accountable to those who have no vote, such as children, persons certified insane and persons serving sentences of imprisonment. It is instructive to consider why so few categories of person are disenfranchised. If people were permanently deprived of the vote as a punishment this could lead to the growth of separate sections of the population whose interests were not catered for and which set themselves against the state. One of the limits upon punishment in a democracy is that it is dangerous to punish a man to such an extent that his children are put at a continuing disadvantage in their relations with their contemporaries. This reduces the chance of their growing up good citizens and stores up trouble for the next generation. A democratic government has to work for good relations between state and citizen in the next generation as well.

The democratic philosophy accepts natural differences between individuals. The ablest citizens have a special obligation to assist in matters of government because it is in everybody's interest that the most important posts should be occupied by the people best able to discharge their responsibilities. On the other hand, it is accepted that people who are sick or are physically or mentally handicapped should be given special assistance. Those who suffer from inherited disorders like diabetes or phenyl-ketonuria are helped as a matter of course. There has been widespread sympathy in Europe for the children who have suffered because their mothers were treated with the drug thalidomide. In the democratic outlook such differences are no basis for regarding people as socially inferior; they are ack-nowledged as conditions calling for special assistance so that the handicapped can play a part in the life of society which can bring them the respect of their peers. Every citizen must con-tribute what he can to the life of the society and must have his particular needs recognised.

Democratic institutions rest upon general acceptance of the proposition that as members of society every voter is equal to every other voter, no matter how different they may be in other respects. It is more difficult to hold the government accountable to the whole electorate when some people are given opportunities denied to others. The privileged defend their advantages, the unprivileged attack them, and the voters think less about their common interests. 'One man, one vote', is a moral principle which is quite separate from the question of natural differences. This is not always recognised, and sometimes it is confused by doctrines which seek to weaken or contradict democratic principles. Two of them are often heard in discussion of racial differences. The first maintains that morality is itself subject to natural laws. The second advances other moral principles as taking priority.

Historically, as Chapter 1 has shown, theories about race as a physical category have often claimed that men of different races were different in their character and therefore should be governed by different laws each suited to the race in question. In 1863 the President of the Anthropological Society of London delivered an address in which he maintained that 'no subject needs more attention at the present time than the position which the Negro race is fitted to hold in Nature. I have said it devolves on the student of the Science of Man to assign each race the position which it shall hold.' Dr James Hunt thought it was cruel for the white man to expect the Negro to accept standards which were beyond his capacity. 'It is painful to reflect on the misery which has been inflicted on the Negro race, from the prevailing ignorance of Anthropological Science, especially as regards the great question of race.' One hundred years later a pamphlet was being circulated in both the United States and England presenting a lecture by Professor Wesley C. George of the School of Medicine in the University of North Carolina in which he argued that if (and only if) 'we can continue to develop a programme of friendly co-operation between the races, with separateness in social life, we can go forward in promoting the talents of the white man and the Negro and can contribute to the welfare and happiness of both'. Like his predecessor, George maintained that social equality would be unfair to black people because they would be unable to compete successfully with whites and failure would make them disappointed and bitter.

The argument of both Hunt and George was that people of Caucasian and Negro stock were of different mental capacity and their ways of life must therefore be different. Their race determined their culture. Doctrines of this kind are called racist. Though the word racism is now often used in a more general fashion its definition in the dictionaries is still that racism denotes a doctrine that racial inheritance determines moral and intellectual qualities. Much of our book has been devoted to explaining how it was that in the nineteenth century some people came mistakenly to formulate such doctrines and others to accept them. We have also tried to show why this was a mistaken theory and to put in its place a more satisfactory explanation of the processes at work in this field. But this is not all. Though Hunt claimed to base his conclusions on 'the general observations of those *unbiased* travellers and others who have been much associated with the Negro race', his own selection of testimony was far from judicious (especially in his use of American sources) and he seems to have been motivated by more than a desire to advance 'Anthropological Science'. There is little excuse for his errors and even less for those of Wesley George. Though racism, strictly defined, arose from scientific error, it was preserved and extended in spite of scientific correction. The private passions of men like Hunt played some part in this, but there were other and less personal influences at work. Why and how racist doctrines were popularised so that they came to gain a hold on the popular mind in Europe and America is an important story, but it is fundamentally different from the one we have tried to tell, and so we have not sought to combine the two.

Those who today advance racist arguments, like Wesley George, draw attention to the higher incidence of crime amongst black Americans than white. They shake their heads sadly over 'the Negroes' standards of social behaviour'. They assume that such differences are the outcome of genetic differences, without looking to see how far they are explicable in terms of income levels, living conditions and so on. High illegitimate birth rates (to which George draws attention) show all sorts of variations of interest to the sociologist. In Bavaria 22 per cent of all children were born out of wedlock in the 1850s (and doubtless many more conceived out of wedlock). Studies by demographers and social statisticians have shown that high illegitimacy rates in many European countries in the last century were attributable to economic and social factors. Legitimacy of birth tends to be emphasised only in those societies in which family connections establish a person's social status. If members of the parental generation have farmland or money to leave to their descendants, legitimate birth is a principle determining rights to inherit. But if a whole sector of society is sunk in poverty with nothing to bequeath and unable to do anything worthwhile to establish members of the new generation, legitimacy matters less. Whenever differences in crime rates and social standards are systematically examined, the reader is led back to sociological considerations.

Hunt sought to persuade others to follow his opinions about 'the Negro's place in nature'. He and some subsequent writers have assumed that Negroes constitute a distinctive race, and that as races are biological units so any discussion about Negro social characteristics must be conducted within a biological framework. We have argued that the category 'Negroes' is not something established on biological principles. Like other racial categories, it is a popular classification influenced by the stereotypes which children learn in their early years. In the United States, as everyone knows, there are 'blacks' so fair-skinned that they can 'pass' as whites, but they are locally known as members of the black community and so identify themselves, often passionately. Definitions of race outside the laboratory are partly political, partly cultural and only partly biological. Claims that moral judgements about races must be based upon biological assessments of their capacity never come to terms with the social nature and biological heterogeneity of racial categories in contemporary society.

The second kind of proposition which obscures the case for treating citizens equally is illustrated by the phrase 'our own people come first'. It does not assert that other groups are racially inferior but that they are to be distinguished as social groups and are less deserving. This argument can be heard in the United States but simpler instances can be found in Britain in connection with the recent immigration of people from the West Indies, India, Pakistan and Bangladesh. Discussing the implications of this movement one Member of Parliament stated, 'the chief difficulty arises from the great influx of unskilled coloured workers of low social standards, of entirely different habits and background and possessing an imperfect knowledge of English'. The disadvantages arising he listed as 'the deplorable housing conditions, the danger to health, the lowering of educational standards, the high incidence of certain crimes, and the social strains caused in the areas where immigrants congregate'. In reply to the claim that their labour was indispensable, he referred to the low productivity of labour in Britain and the need to economise in the use of labour by mechanisation. There was room for argument about the factual basis of every one of these assertions but to quarrel with them was to accept the speaker's definition of what 'the problem' was. He wished to represent it as a question of immigration whereas by the time he spoke the flow of immigrants had been reduced to a trickle and the basic problem was that of race relations, of how Britain was to respond to the social consequences of an economic policy which welcomed black immigrants who were willing to do Britain's dirty jobs. Part of the problem was the prejudice of white English people. After all, it is desirable to reduce colour prejudice and anti-semitism in a country whether or not there are many blacks and Jews about; prejudice is a sign of poor mental health in a community. (Prejudice is other things too, and in so far as it is a response to real conflicts, one needs to explain why the true nature of these conflicts is not appreciated.) The politician sought to keep out of the debate any consideration of irrational hostility; to accept the often hasty assumptions of his 'own people' as a starting point for policy; and to present the issues as calling for a decision about immigration.

In the United States, during the last thirty years, there has been a major migration of black people from the cotton counties of the South to cities and to the North. One calculation showed that in southern Arkansas the introduction of just one tractor meant the displacement of 100 people, farm workers and their dependants, mostly black. There was no other work for them so they had to come north, to Chicago, Detroit or another big city, to take work if available or to live on relief. Unlike the black people in the British cities there could be no talk of 'they should not have been allowed to come' or 'they should be sent back', instead the white Americans were the more ready to see them as a distinct ethnic group because the whites in many cases thought of themselves as Italian-Americans, Polish-Americans, Irish-Americans, Jewish-Americans and so on.

If a nation says 'this is our country' and restricts immigration, that is its right. If a group says 'we will observe our civic obligations but in our religious observance, our marriages and social patterns most of us want to remain a distinct community', that too is its right. But once a group of immigrants have been admitted they and their children must become socially equal citizens if the processes of democracy are not to be upset. If a minority wishes to lead a separate private life its children must not be prevented from forsaking their parents' customs and joining the majority if that is their wish. In this connection it is worth reflecting on why modern nations have laws saying that children of certain ages must attend school. There may well be religious groups which do not wish their children to attend school or to attend only special schools. If such parents were allowed to keep their children at home so that they did not learn to read and write or to function as citizens, this would doubtless cause a lot of inconvenience to other people. The obligations of citizenship set the limits within which minorities may be separate. They also define the duty of the majority towards the minority citizens of the next generation.

Arguments which make appeal to feelings about 'our own people' are often much more subtle than those which employ racist notions. When advanced by prominent people they may have the effect of reinforcing popular prejudices even though the speaker has used words which, on the surface, seem neutral. The point to be watched is that arguments are addressed to the present generation, suggesting that one section of the electorate deserves preference. In this way it obscures the consequences for the next generation. Political life in that generation will fall further short of the democratic ideal if some citizens are at a disadvantage because their parents had to live in inferior neighbourhoods and they themselves were handicapped from the cradle. A democracy has no place for second-class citizens because there can be no second-class votes. When people like the Member of Parliament just quoted talk in terms of 'we British people in our over-crowded island' contrasting 'us' with 'them', 'we British' with 'these immigrants', they polarise the situation along one line of division, causing some of their audience to overlook the bonds of occupation, political outlook, religion, leisure interests and so on which unite people in different colour categories. They choose to emphasise the immigrant status of the first generation when it is of great importance to consider the citizenship status which their children—most of whom are not immigrants—will acquire at eighteen years of age.

The first of the two kinds of argument we have just discussed periodically draws new life from scientific discoveries. The appeal to scientific authority is ever more frequent, for technological achievements have brought scientific thought a reputation for validity shared by no other body of ideas in modern society. As a result, apparent social implications of scientific propositions have been examined with great concern, and interest groups have sought to show, wherever possible, that scientific findings were on 'their side'. This has often affected debates about race. Those who drafted the first UNESCO Statement on Race wished to testify that racism enjoyed no scientific support. Those who opposed the desegregation decisions of the US Supreme Court tried to prove that they were based on incorrect and incomplete biological knowledge. Both sides have, in effect, maintained that their opponents' political beliefs were not merely amoral but unnatural as well; biological facts had implications, and the only valid political beliefs were those which were logically derived from scientific fact.

This kind of debate has not drawn a sufficiently clear distinction between scientific knowledge and the process by which citizens choose the sort of social pattern they prefer. Scientific findings may be important in knowing how to create a particular kind of society, what means will be effective and what particular policies might cost in various ways, but they cannot determine what the ends of society should be. Natural differences do not necessitate social inequalities. If one man is more clever than another this does not of itself mean that he ought to have two votes. It does not mean that he should be given a longer and more expensive period of education which is paid for largely by fellow citizens who are less clever. Nothing in scientific knowledge says that a society should not handicap the clever and give extra assistance to the dull-witted so that everyone would perform similarly on a comprehension test. Scientific knowledge does suggest, however, that the costs of such a policy would be enormous and that no such society could enjoy the standard of living that the contemporary European and North American takes for granted.

Seen from this standpoint, there is no reason for agitation about the widespread conclusion of scientists that human beings differ from one another in IQ for genetic reasons (though not only for genetic reasons). Such a conclusion does not mean that people of different IQ should be socially unequal. Whether or not social inequality should be geared to IQ is a political issue having nothing to do with the heritability of IQ. Nor do the scientific findings show that IQ differences arise from sources beyond the control of men. Some of the variation derives from inequalities in present social patterns and governments are not obliged to maintain these patterns even though some electors may take them for granted. It is possible to envisage government policies which, by changing these patterns, could reduce IQ variation in the society. Governmental action could improve the environments in which there are concentrations of people with low IQ; people could be transferred between such environments and those with residents of high IQ; or spending on health, education and social services could be changed to the benefit of the poor neighbourhoods. If it were widely agreed that genetic factors were involved in particular cases of low IQ, the government could encourage a lower birth rate in the relevant low IQ sector of the population. Many people today would probably consider such policies unacceptable, but this is nevertheless a political choice, and there is plenty of evidence to suggest that Europeans and North Americans are much less tolerant of some kinds of social inequality today than they were a century ago. They already support many measures designed to restrain or reduce other kinds of inequality.

The direction of our argument should by now be clear, but there is one issue on which there must be no room for misunderstanding. If it could be firmly established that blacks, Irishmen, Protestants, Catholics, men or women etc had lower average measured intelligence for genetic reasons, what could be done about it? We should remember firstly that in the case of racial differences, at least, the IQ gap is not categorical. It is not the case that *all* yellows score above *all* whites who score above *all* blacks. The lower average IQ scores of black Americans cannot legitimately be interpreted as evidence of general 'inferiority' or even of intellectual inferiority. Jensen himself has emphasised that 'it is nonsense to speak of different racial gene pools in general as superior or inferior'. Such evaluative terms are meaningful only in reference to a particular trait and the degree of adaptation to a particular environment which this trait permits. IQ tests measure only one part of overall mental ability, and Jensen's own research shows that on tests of at least one other type of mental ability black Americans score as well as, or better than, whites. Secondly, even if the IQ gap is partly genetic, it does not follow that it is unalterable. In Chapter 4 we discussed possible means whereby environmental intervention could reduce or eliminate a group phenotypic difference. Also, as we know from Chapter 3, the gene pools of populations can change substantially within a few generations under strong selective pressures, natural or artificial. Therefore, though we do not ourselves endorse any particular scheme for eugenic engineering (eg selective birth control), we observe that this sort of measure could help to eliminate a genetic IQ gap.

Closer consideration suggests therefore that the question about group differences in average IQ is not so very different from the question about individual differences. Some blacks score well above the white average and some whites well above the yellow average. While it is with individuals that any policy must ultimately deal, the problems are usually not ultimate but proximate, and in the present day mental ability differences may be associated with groups of people who are distinctive in particular ways and live in particular localities. In so far as average group differences in IQ contribute to discrimination, to unrest, and to the alienation of disadvantaged groups from a society which chooses to reward persons according to IQ, social justice might be served by trying to reduce IQ differences.

The majority of the population needs to understand the arguments in favour of such policies. These will be more successful if they are sensitive to the social factors patterning minority communities. If the people of a neighbourhood are told that they are getting extra resources because the government regards them as a problem, they are less likely to use those resources in the manner intended than if they are told that they have a right to them. Self-confidence and pride of belonging can be more important than a new classroom. Therefore it may well be desirable to provide extra assistance to groups living in the sorts of neighbourhood that become poverty traps.

We have argued that no major social implications automatically flow from biological findings, and that therefore the meaning people come to attach to racial differences depends upon political decisions. This helps explain the pattern of racial discrimination in the world today. But it is well to remember that discrimination is itself a complex phenomenon that can spring from varied sources. One of us has suggested in another book, *Racial Minorities*, that the causes of discrimination fall into four categories. We will explain them briefly, mentioning their implication for the discussion of race as a factor which complicates efforts to build a more democratic society. Discrimination is a kind of behaviour, in which a person is treated differently because he is placed in a particular social category. Often discrimination is the expression of a prejudiced attitude on someone's part but this is not always the case, and in some circumstances prejudiced people do not discriminate because there are other considerations which discourage them from doing so. For example, they may be afraid of the consequences. Though discrimination and prejudice are distinct concepts which are more useful if they are not confounded, the behaviour and attitudes which they define often go together in practice. Each strengthens the other.

The first element which may be present in discrimination is that of personality weakness. Some people for one reason or another do not have well-balanced personalities; they need to make up for their own deficiencies by releasing their aggression on to some suitable scapegoat. If one scapegoat is driven out into the desert they are going to need another so that some policy is called for which will result in a better level of mental health. This is not simply a matter for psychiatrists in mental hospitals. Politicians sometimes advance their own ends by encouraging attacks on scapegoats. Equally they can pursue policies which aim at maximising harmony between groups, relaxing tensions and encouraging neighbourliness. We do not suggest that people should be made to love one another, but simply observe that some social policies make it easier for them not to hate rival groups so much.

The second element is that of ethnocentrism, which is a tendency to prefer people from one's own nation, to see things from the standpoint of that nation, and to set a lower value on other nations. Ethnocentrism is different from the prejudice that stems from personality weakness in that it is less irrational and can be modified by education or favourable experience of the nations previously regarded as alien.

A third element is role-determined discrimination. It is found when people occupy social roles in which they believe they are expected to discriminate. The landlord who turns away a would-be coloured tenant by saying, 'I don't mind, but the neighbours would object', may not be telling the whole truth, but when there is truth in its explanation it provides an example of the way some kinds of discrimination are tied to particular situations.

The fourth element has already been introduced. It is opportunism. It frequently happens that politicians and others appeal to ethnocentric or prejudiced attitudes in order to advance their own ends. So long as particular groups can be presented as scapegoats this possibility will remain open. It points to an additional reason for seeking to eliminate social inequalities and sounds a warning that social and economic differences which are identified with racial differences are likely to evoke extra strong emotions.

Racial antagonism has its roots in social and psychological factors of this kind. It is not an inevitable feature which must be fatalistically accepted. Though it is improbable that racial antagonism can ever be reduced to absolute zero it is not difficult, looking round the world, to see that it is higher in some places than others and to remember that it goes up and down in intensity. If men were agreed that they wished to reduce it, and were prepared to put the reduction of tension higher in their priorities relative to the short-term pursuit of individual gain, they could substantially reduce the emotion that goes with racial labels. As we argued in Chapter 5, the causes of tension are not primarily biological, so men must look behind the labels at the social sources of antagonism and act so as to discourage or penalise discriminatory behaviour. Education has an important part to play in such a programme but by itself it can do little. It is small use trying to teach children in school to adopt a view of racial differences sharply at variance with that obtaining outside the school, in the homes, on the streets, at places of work. For even if children could be brought to accept the teachers' views while at school, the prospects of their keeping to them for long in situations where the pressures go in a contrary direction are not encouraging. Educational policies need to be seen as part of a programme for seeking greater democracy in a social situation which includes some forces pulling in the opposite direction.

It is easy to detect weaknesses in the social systems which claim to be democratic. Much that appears inefficient is excused as inherent in democratic procedures. Democracy requires constant education of those who have to judge what is done in their name. Democracy is threatened today on many sides: by the complexity of huge organisations like multi-national companies and government bureaucracies which are unresponsive to the individual citizen; by the political ambitions of nation states; by the impatience of those so convinced of the verdict of history that they believe the end justifies the means. But when considering the criticisms and threats the citizen will always have to contemplate the alternatives. For as modern democracies fall short of the ideal, it is difficult to discover any other political system which is not open to far more serious objections.

The historical period in which the concept of race attracted attention was one in which democracy was gaining new adherents in Europe and was increasingly inspiring political programmes both there and in the United States. Doctrines of racism implied that democracy was right for white people, subordination and benevolent despotism for coloured races. That period is over. The race concept was in its early years used as a weapon by the West against the economically less developed parts of the world. It will not be surprising if the people in those other parts, now they have organised themselves as nations, use racial identifications as a weapon against the West. The honourable course for western peoples is to strive for more democracy on a world scale to cope with problems which increasingly relate to the worldwide network which international trade and politics have been building with mounting speed during the past century.

FURTHER READING

To check on many of our statements or to explore their implications the reader would need access to academic journals that are usually available only in university libraries. In suggesting further reading we have limited our list to books, as these can be obtained with less difficulty. We have included some books of which we ourselves are critical.

Chapter 1
Barzun, Jacques. *Race: A Study in Superstition.* New York: Harper, 1965
Curtin, Philip D. *The Image of Africa: British Ideas and Action, 1780–1850.* Madison, Wis: University of Wisconsin Press; London: Macmillan, 1964
Greene, J. C. *The Death of Adam: Evolution and Its Impact on Western Thought.* New York: Mentor Books, 1959
Mason, Philip. *Prospero's Magic: Some Thoughts on Class and Race.* London: Oxford University Press, 1962
Stocking, George W. *Race, Culture and Evolution: Essays in the History of Anthropology.* New York: Free Press, 1968

Chapter 2
King, James. *The Biology of Race.* New York: Harcourt Brace Jovanovich, 1971
Lerner, I. Michael. *Heredity, Evolution and Society.* San Francisco, Calif: W. H. Freeman, 1968
Montagu, Ashley (ed). *The Concept of Race.* New York and London: Collier-Macmillan, 1964

Chapter 3
Dobzhansky, Theodosius. *Mankind Evolving.* New Haven, Conn: Yale University Press, 1962

Garn, Stanley (ed). *Readings on Race*. Springfield, Ill: Thomas, 2nd ed 1968

Montagu, Ashley (ed). *Culture and the Evolution of Man*. New York: Oxford University Press, 1962

Osborne, Richard (ed). *The Biological and Social Meaning of Race*. San Francisco, Calif: W. H. Freeman, 1971

Russell, W. M. S. and Claire. *Violence, Monkeys and Man*. London: Macmillan, 1968

Chapter 4

Brace, C. Loring, Gamble, G. R. and Bond, J. T. (eds). *Race and Intelligence*. Washington, DC: American Anthropological Association. Anthropological Studies No 8, 1971

Eysenck, H. J. *Race, Intelligence and Education*. London: Temple Smith, 1971. US edition: *The IQ Argument*. Freeport, NY: Library Press, 1971

Jensen, A. R. *et al*. *Environment, Heredity and Intelligence*. Cambridge, Mass: Harvard Educational Review Reprint Series No 2, 1969

Richardson, R., Spears, D. and Richards, M. (eds). *Race, Culture and Intelligence*. Harmondsworth, Middx: Penguin, 1972

Chapter 5

Glass, D. C. (ed). *Genetics*. New York: Rockefeller University Press and Russell Sage Foundation, 1968

Mead, Margaret, Dobzhansky, Theodosius, Tobach, Ethel and Light, Richard (eds). *Science and the Concept of Race*. New York: Columbia University Press, 1968

Montagu, Ashley (ed). *Man and Aggression*. London and New York: Oxford University Press, 2nd ed 1973

The quotations in chapter 4 (in order of appearance) are from H. J. Eysenck, *Know Your Own IQ*, Penguin, 1962, pp 8 and 33; and A. R. Jensen's article in *Environment, Heredity and Intelligence*, op cit, pp 59–60, 82, 78, 90 and 98

INDEX